THE NEIGHBORHOOD GANG

The Neighborhood Gang

Memoirs of the 70s: A Decade of Change

D.L. TRACEY

Badb Publishing

Contents

ISBN: 979-8-218-24567-2 (Paperback)
ISBN: 979-8-218-24835-2 (Hardcover)

Library of Congress Control Number: 2024908161

The events in the book are my memories from my perspective. Certain names have been changed to protect the identities of those involved.

Front cover image by Elite Authors.
Book design by Ingram Spark.
Printed by Badb Publishing, in the United States of America.
First printing edition 2024.
Ingram Spark Printing
La Vergne, Tennessee 37086

www.dltracey.com

dltraceybooks@gmail.com

Dedicated to:

Mr. Nick {The Man} Rello
Mr. Skip {The Music}Tuttle
&
Mr. Richard {The Hot Rod} Smith
Miss each of you very much every day.
Till we all meet again.

Preface

Growing Up in the Seventies

On the Quest to Be Wicked Cool perfectly summarizes how my friends and I in Weymouth woke up each morning so many years ago. But so much more was happening in our world, changes that would shape the lives of future generations.

Space Invaders launched a craze for video games. Families marveled at the miracle of Pong. The first ever cellular mobile phone made its appearance in the world. The electronic calculator showed us that we didn't need to learn math; we only had to work for three weeks to buy one. The microwave oven made it easier to cook something at night when you came home wicked high and the last thing you wanted was your parents watching you cook on a gas stove.

Saturday Night Fever showed some of us a new way to dance. *Animal House* led most of us to a new way to laugh. George Lucas showed us a movie called *Star Wars*, about how to dream and wish. *Jaws* made it impossible to swim in the ocean again. *Monty Python and the Holy Grail,* do I need to say more about this classic? These and many more movies playing in theaters and drive-ins would help shape the future.

"We Will Rock You" by Queen was at the top of the charts. Judas Priest gave birth to a new term, "You've Got Another Thing Comin'." Kansas showed us the *Point of Know Return.* Pink Floyd took us to *The Dark Side of The Moon.* Andrew Gold was such "A Lonely Boy." REO Speedwagon taught us to "Roll with the Changes." Fleetwood Mac took us to our "Dreams" (love you, Tina). Marshall Tucker asked us to "see love."

The seventies were a massive decade for music and drugs. *Music was everywhere.* The rock and roll genre that started in the sixties continued to improve and flourish, crashing like a runaway train into the seventies. What had been an oddity became a way of life. This music changed how we saw everything.

All sorts of rock sub-genres emerged, and much of this loud music with indistinguishable lyrics had our parents shaking their heads and wondering what would become of us kids if we kept listening to it. All across Weymouth, parents yelled up to our rooms, "Turn that shit down!"

Aerosmith was the most powerful gang of rock 'n' roll outlaws that music has ever seen—or will ever see. As Beavis and Butt-Head said, "There are none better." This band set the stage for what rock would become and inspired many subsequent rock artists. To this day, "Sweet Emotion" is the song of songs when it comes to the bad boys of Boston. *You're telling me things, but your girlfriend lied.*

The Cars came late in the seventies but were *just what we needed.* If you think about it, I mean, wow. Nothing about the Cars was extraordinary, but their first five albums all went certified platinum. This band outta Boston somehow transgressed the rock 'n' roll code and gave us a new type of sound, wave/ power pop, but they were wicked cool anyway.

Boston wasn't a "real" band like other, more traditional bands. You could say they were merely a studio creation of founder and MIT geek Tom Scholz. Well, maybe. But those nerds created "More Than a Feeling," one of the greatest songs not only of the seventies, but of all time. You can't argue that —not in this town, anyway. Plus, "Amanda"? Come on, man. That shit is as real as it gets. Boston was the first band to debut at Madison Square Garden in New York City. I would buy any album from Boston without even hearing it first.

The J. Geils Band, *outta Woostah*, was America's pre-eminent party band. Responsible for ear-wormy chart-toppers like "Centerfold," "Freeze Frame," and "Love Stinks," Geils played R&B-influenced rock during the seventies and beyond. No one loved (or understood) rock 'n' roll better than these guys. Trust me on this one. *I don't care for any Casanova thing. All I can say is...* (You know the words, Wally P. Finish this for me.)

There were a hell of a lot more bands that we Weymouth folks cherished. Groups like Talking Heads, Steely Dan, Led Zeppelin, the Grateful Dead, and the Who, to name a few, filled endless hours of late-night listening while we smoked *the weed*. This combination had all of us pondering our very existence. We'd listen to songs like "Green Grass and High Tides" by the Outlaws and contemplate such heady lines as "a rainbow grew around the sun." (Thinking of you, Ginny S. How many beers did we drink together? How many joints did we share? Not enough. Youth is complicated.)

The sixties broke down the fashion barriers and paved the way for the wild seventies. For women, skirts got shorter, as did shorts. It was the decade of the hot pants (extremely short shorts). Most girls were trying to get *Charlie's Angels* hair-dos. Brightly colored bell bottoms and blousy shirts were the clothes of choice early on, but such hippie garb soon gave way to the disco look, anything from miniskirts to midi skirts to halter-neck catsuits with tropical and exotic prints. Jeans also became part of the teenage norm for both sexes, suitable for all occasions except highly formal ones.

Fashion for us guys moved swiftly. It started with hippie garb and morphed into ripped jeans and rock T-shirts topped with unbuttoned plaid flannel shirts. Bell bottoms were still fashionable, and platform shoes were worn for more formal affairs. Otherwise, sneakers were the footwear of choice for both sexes.

Pet Rocks didn't need to be fed, walked, or bathed, making them the best pets ever, and mood rings were all the rage. All your friends knew to stay away when the ring suddenly turned black because you were in a bad mood. Eight-track tapes and cassettes brought your brand of music to your car, the new way to listen to music in your vehicle. You could hear the same song for hours without worrying when the radio station would play it again. I wore shoes that improved my posture. The lowered heels forced me to walk straighter, or so the thought went.

We stayed up wicked late—and usually high—to watch some of the first episodes of *Saturday Night Live* back when it was wicked funny. ("Can you say, "Gas shortage"?) So many of the original cast members are now gone, but they took comedy to a new level of laughter and took us to a new level of high and outright weird in a fun way.

"I may be gone, but rock and roll lives on." ~ John Belushi
(1949–1982)

Maybe one of the saddest deaths of our youth was that of an American actor, comedian, and singer, one of Saturday Night Live's seven original cast members. For kids of the seventies, his name will always be synonymous with a new brand of on-and-over-the-edge comedy. From his spot-on impression of Joe Cocker to his hilarious performances as Samurai Futaba, John "Bluto" Belushi cemented his place as one of the best at his trade.

I sifted through thousands of musical memories while creating this memoir of the seventies and our youth. As I listened to bands from Aerosmith to ZZ Top, I experienced the days of our childhood all over again, and I encourage you to do the same while you read this book.

Like a storm, time rolls on. Feel our laughter, love, pain, friendships, and so much more as you slowly turn the pages and remember your own childhood with a smile and a few tears.

Yes, these are my memories, but my hope is that everyone can put themselves in the pictures I have painted.

Nowhere were the seventies more real than in a small coastal town in Massachusetts called Weymouth. I tell people that the seventies were born in this small town of our youth. Yes, we, the youth of Weymouth, set the stage for future generations. Our style and passion for drugs, music, and living on the edge of the universe will never be matched. And remember, George D., what Frank Zappa told us all: *Watch out where the huskies go, and don't you eat that yellow snow.*

So, our story begins. ~ trace

Chapter One

July 1978

This Place Was Called Home

So much hatred for this place called home. Never was over the years. It never felt like home. The viciousness of a mother and sisters was overwhelming at times. A drunk father who found the time in a bar chair and stinger drinks was of more comfort than family life. A mother who spent her time chasing another man, forsaking her husband's namesake son because of a name. Yes, the mother invented child abuse. But I realize now that it was because of her husband's abuse and the inability to fight back that she took it out on his named son daily.

Sixty-five years later, I forgive you. Don't you dare be so petty or smug that you think this is for you. This is not for you but for my soul, heart, sanity, and hatred. I will no longer allow you to pollute my heart with bitterness, fear, distrust, or anger like mordacious chains shackling me to the painful past. I forgive you because my intense hate and childhood fear of you is just another way of holding on, and you don't belong here anymore.

~ child two of five

North Weymouth, Massachusetts. For one warm night in July, my parents' home would become an outdoor music venue. Over three hundred-plus teens were about to descend upon the small backyard of the home on Frank Rd. It would be a night of Tracey family graduations, with three parties at once: little brother Glenn from a local high, little sister Susan from nursing school, and little sister Kim from a local grade school. All three graduation classes, along with family and friends, had been invited to attend.

At least, that was the plan.

As I sit and write this story of our adolescent years in the endless early morning hours, I realize now that this night was the end of my tyeenage years. This was the summer when the real world started. It was the end of something and the beginning of something else, as I love to say about life.

My mother had asked Joe to bring over the band and play for the night. The band consisted of a few of my friends from the neighborhood, Joe, Ryan, Lucas, Todd, and Parker, and I called it the Neighborhood Band. They had agreed to play for free due to our friendship and my mother's many years of putting up with late-night chess matches between Joe and me at her dining room table.

As the band prepared on my mother's back porch, the crowd of kids swelled and overflowed into the neighbors' yards and beyond. Sitting over in the corner of my parents' yard with my long-time and much older girlfriend Liz W., yours truly was home on leave from the Marines and looking forward to spending some time with my friends after the show.

Little brother Glenn stood nervously on my parents' back porch, microphone in hand, preparing to address the crowd and introduce the band for one rocking night. The audience had now grown to over three hundred. Every inch of the yard was covered with teens of all shapes and sizes. The hill in the backyard with a wall of boulders, built by my grandfather many years ago, made a perfect place to sit and watch the show.

"Hello!" Glenn shouted out to the crowd, which included some of Weymouth's finest, meanest, drunkest, highest, shyest, and every other type of kid you could think of.

With a tremendous roar, the crowd replied, "Hey, Glenn!" along with hoots and hollers. "Start the show!"

"Enjoy the show!"

Glenn walked away from the microphone, and Joe stepped forward with a cigarette dangling from his lips and a guitar hanging from his shoulder. The rest of the band took their places behind him. Joe looked out at the crowd and saw me in the corner of the yard, with Liz's head nestling against my shoulder and Bud bottles in our hands. Then, in typical Joe style, he took one more drag of his cigarette and stuck the burning butt into the top of his guitar so he could smoke the rest of it later.

He looked out over the crowd again, nodded, pointed, and smiled at a few group members. When he turned back toward me, Liz and I paused momentarily as if we both knew the years of our youth were behind us. We were laughing and living, drinking, smoking, and wishing. This was the turning point to the next journey in our lives.

Then Joe did what he always did when he started a show. "Hey, Trace! Listen to this," he yelled out over the endless sea of kids. The band started playing "China Grove" by the Doobie Brothers. The crowd of teens went wild, dancing and singing along. Joe and the group had changed the words from "China Grove" to "Weymouth, Massachusetts," and the crowd went wild.

The sky was wicked clear, and the stars had come down from the heavens to shine their spotlights on the concert and the rites of our passage in life, the perfect backdrop as we followed the music, sailing into the night, touching everything for miles.

I watched the crowd as the band played "Sail Away" by Styx. *We climbed aboard their starship; we headed for the skies.*

Looking around, I could see and smell lit joints (Mary Jane) all over my parents' backyard. For some reason, on this night, my dad was okay with all the pot smoking in his yard. He stayed in front of the house, trying to keep the crowd orderly, which continued to flow from all over Weymouth onto Frank Rd. Two police officers and a Weymouth selectman attempted to lend a hand with the overwhelming sea of kids descending on the music. It was as if the Pied Piper of Hamelin himself were casting an eerie spell that night, pulling in the sea of kids to that special place and moment of music.

On the other hand, my mother sat off to the side of the back porch, enjoying the night with my little sister and about a dozen of her friends from school and their parents.

This concert was to become a night to remember for some and a night never to be remembered for too many, and it seemed everyone wanted to be part of the history of this night in any fashion. Even now, so many years later, all this is a vivid memory of sadness and changes in my life. In all our lives, I am willing to bet.

The band kicked into high gear and started playing "Surrender" by Cheap Trick: *Rolling numbers, rock and rolling, got my Kiss records out.* Then the crowd of teens went *on a stormy sea of moving emotion* as "Carry on Wayward Son" by Kansas filled the night air. The band was rocking, and so was everyone else, deep into the night...

Little did I know that the end of my youth was upon me that night.

"Well, I feel so good; everybody's getting high," Joe sang, looking over toward Liz and me.

"I'm so glad we made it! I'm so glad we made it!" I yelled back, tipping my beer in acknowledgment. The song was "Gimme Some Lovin'" by the Spencer Davis Group. But that didn't matter; it was about the night and the gang's friendship. It was a song for all of us. We were trashed and rocking.

Nuzzling closer to me, Liz whispered in my ear as she gently stroked my thigh with her hand, "You two are great friends." Was this a sign of things to come? *You better take it easy 'cause the place is on fire.* She took a hit from a joint passed to her by someone sitting next to us and kissed me deeply, slowly passing the smoke to me.

"Don't you think that love can last?" Joe sang out. *Maybe she's in need of a kiss.* Not wanting to let go of that kiss, I clutched her tightly, pulling in as much smoke as possible. Her hand was still stroking my thigh. Oh, we were getting *wicked* high.

The summer of 1978 was upon us. Memories filled the night with each song. "Smoke on the Water" by Deep Purple had the crowd believing in forever: *Swiss time was running out. It seemed that we would lose the race.* The band continued to rock for hours. "Stairway to Heaven" by Led Zeppelin called all of us to our future: *Our head is humming, and it won't go; if you don't know, the piper's calling you to join him.* "Psycho Killer" by the Talking Heads had the crowd jumping. Joe wore a creepy mask as he sang, "Psycho killer, qu'est-ce que c'est?"

"Time Has Come Today" by the Chamber Brothers reminded us what life could do to us if we let it end: *I've been crushed by a tumbling tide (time), and my soul has been psychedeelicized (time).* I always wonder if the song was about the sixties ending or where my life was heading. It turns out it was my life for the next ten years. Words can have such meaning that we need to listen to.

The lost years of my life were quickly approaching. Soon time would take me on a life-and-death struggle around the world. Homelessness, drugs, and alcohol became my travel companions. This night was my sendoff party for a journey that would last for the next ten years.

Thankfully, over the lost years, the need to blow out the candle of my life never happened. Years later, my life would be saved by a six-year-old boy who would become my son. But that's another story. Love you, son of mine.

Late into the night, we danced and sang the songs of our youth. Finally, the police showed up and closed down the party of our past. Looking back now, I know this was the end of our adolescence.

After the show, Liz and I grabbed a few beers and blankets and headed down to a special late-night place many of us knew where we would not be bothered. I am sure many of you are smiling and nodding now because you know of this place. Yes, that place was Wessagusset Beach. But if it was cold up on Great Hill, the back seat of your car tended to work just fine.

Anyone who has ever been there at night during the warm months understands the beauty that comes with this part of our world. The quiet of the ocean, as it sleeps, is overwhelming. The chugging of fishing boats heading out to sea and the crashing of small waves on the New England shore break the quiet stillness of the night.

With blankets and beers in hand, we headed to the far end of the beach, where the jetty divides the old and new beach. We planned to watch the sunrise together. Laying one blanket on the soft sand, we sat on it and wrapped the other around us for warmth. Then we softly sang "More Than a Feeling" by Boston: *When I hear that old song they used to play.*

Yes, it was more than a feeling that was coming over me. I was in love with this woman and all that she was. Looking back now, after all these years, I realize she was my first real love. We had been dating for several months, but my time in the service had kept us apart a few months at a time.

I met her during my first apartment time. We worked the late shift at a local fast-food joint on Bridge St. Back in the day, I had no car, so she would give me the ten-mile ride to my place on Winter St. each night in a beat-up old car called the Purple Ghost. On nights we didn't work together, I would thumb the long journey home on Weymouth's quiet streets, talking to myself the whole time. What a dope I was.

Liz lit a doobie, inhaled deeply, and passed the joint to me. "Wow, what a night," she murmured, exhaling the thick white smoke into the early morning ocean breeze. Yes, what a night. Holding the smoke in for a moment, I could feel the buzz coming over me, warming me. As I handed the joint back to her, I thought of the strawberry-blonde woman next to me, ten years my senior.

Her milky white skin was soft as we kissed slowly, and her tongue probed deeply. Her eyes were the color of green jade. The moonlight danced in her eyes as they peered into my soul, promising a sweet, passionate night. I wanted this to last forever.

"You and your friends have such a special friendship," she said, taking another deep hit from the joint. She kissed me again, forcing the harsh smoke deep into my lungs. *All right now, baby, it's all right now* played somewhere off in my memory of the night gone by.

"Tell me, Trace, about your friendship with all your friends." She handed the joint back to me and then gently stroked my face. Her other hand slowly moved under my shirt. "I saw it tonight. There is something special about all of this." She lay back on the blanket and looked up at me. A line from "Chevy Van" by Sammy Johns invaded my thoughts: *'Cause, like a picture, she was laying there, moonlight dancing off her hair.*

This woman was beautiful in every way. As I watched every move on her face, the music came back to me, "All Right Now" by Free: *Don't you think that love can last?* Yes, we were all right now, and our love would last.

"Maybe someday," I said, pulling this beautiful woman with long strawberry hair toward me as I lay beside her on the blanket.

I never got around to telling her about my friendships with Joe, Jim, Oats, Tina, and the rest of the gang until many years later.

All right now, baby, it's a-all right now.
All right now, baby, it's a-all right now.
~ Free, "All right now"

Our story continues ~ trace

Chapter Two

Summer of 2009

A good life has maybe eighty years until it crumbles with
age.
You only have so much life until it's gone with the years.
A trip to the past is my endless hurt of times gone by,
'Cause, as the young years wear on, they take us to the get-
ting-old years.
Yeah, sooner or later, time does take a huge toll on the years.
That I could look at my whole life and try not to cry.
Life was meant only to last so long, stories of our lives.
Do memories of my life last forever?
Sometimes life gets the best of us.
How many times did I pick myself up off the floor?
The bounce of getting back up quickly is gone,
'Cause, as the young years wear on, they take us to the get-
ting-old years.
Maybe now are the important years.
I wish you were now always.
You only have so much life until it's gone with the years.
~ trace

In the summer of 2009, my little brother Glenn decided to get married. My beautiful wife, Lori, and I journeyed from the great state of Tex-ass to the shores of Cape Cod. For Lori, this would be her first trip to New England.

A few days before the wedding, she asked me to show her around all my old haunts and where I had grown up. "Hey, Trace, how about a trip? Show me where you grew up." This request, for some reason, caught me by surprise. Sometimes I am pretty sure I have yet to grow up.

I'd never really talked to her, or anyone else, about my past and tended to stick to vagueness when describing my younger life. But I couldn't see any way out of it, so I said, "Sure. Let's go." I opened the car door, she climbed in, and off we drove from the present to my past.

A trip to Weymouth was at hand. Frank Rd., where I grew up, McCulloch, Bicknell, Weymouth North High, jumping off the Hingham Bridge, a slow walk up the rez to Reversing Falls— all were part of the journey of my mixed-up past. It would be a trip to the old neighborhood, or, as Lori called it, a *telephone pole in the woods*. Me, I called it growing up. Kinda.

As I turned the rental car onto Katherine St., REO Speedwagon's "Roll with the Changes" played softly on the radio: *Until you poured on me like a sweet sun shower.* I slowed down as the memories started to surface, making me dizzy or excited to return to my youth. Looking down at the street, I could see three kids standing around the entrance to the woods. I pulled the car to a stop a few feet from them, and they turned and headed into the woods. One of them paused momentarily and looked toward me as I slowly climbed out of the car and into my memories.

"Hey, Trace, ya coming?" It was Jim, my old friend, all of sixteen years old, so full of life, dressed in faded jeans, sneakers, a T-shirt, and a red-and-black-checkered flannel shirt (the first actual untucked shirts began in Weymouth in the seventies), calling me back to my memories. Back to all our memories.

He took one more hit of his cigarette, dropped the still-lit stub to the ground, and blew the smoke into the air. Then, with a smile and a nod, he walked through the gray haze into the woods.

Lori got out of the car and took my arm, and we strolled into the woods. A few yards in, the trees opened into a clearing. The downed pole, forty years later, still lay on one side of the clearing. So many years had passed since it had fallen. How many times had I sat on that log with the gang and gotten wasted? Many of our initials, carved into the fallen pole, were still visible, though they had faded over the years. That day, though, they seemed fresh and new to me, like the day they were carved.

Lori moved closer, wrapped her arms tightly around me, and laid her head softly against my chest. "What do you see, Trace?" Her question was soft and to the point. I smiled a bit; yes, my beautiful wife understood me as an author and knew I was seeing a story of life. Or was it memories of my life or all of our lives? "Back to Paradise" by 38 Special whispered in my mind: *Old Saint Peter at the pearly gate... Take me back to paradise.*

Slowly at first, friends from my youth began their journey to the neighborhood once again, as we'd done daily so many years ago. Joe, Tina, Jim, Oats, and every one of the gang was there. "Trace, finally! Where ya been?" Joe called out as we stepped through the gray haze into the seventies of our youth.

"Been busy with life, but I am here now," I whispered to my friend as he took a wicked-big hit of the joint Mark had handed him. Was it moments ago or so many years ago? Puff, his head exploded in the gray smoke of his high as he exhaled. Like I was viewing some old black-and-white film, I watched and smiled, but it was a sad smile.

Flashback to the grooviest of times. Fleetwood Mac's "Silver Springs" slowly played. It seemed as if I had watched a moment of my past play out before me. *Time cast its spell on you, but you won't forget me.* The warmth of past friendships settled on me like a gentle New England breeze coming off the Atlantic on a bright summer morning. The smell of home-grown pot filled the air. The taste of Budweiser filled my mouth. Was I getting high on my memories?

Though Lori could not see any of this, she could feel it. "Paint it, Trace. Paint it just for me," she whispered ever so softly to me, tightening her grasp on my body.

Turning toward her, I caught sight of my wife, young and seventeen. I had seen many pictures of her in her youth, but her beauty in life made me hope we would be together forever. I touched her cheek softly. "You are as beautiful today as you were in your youth." Tears fell slowly down her cheeks as she turned back to listen and see the memories of her youth.

We watched the canvas come alive as I smiled and began to paint with words. It was a sad smile of memories past, of a time of hope, a time of youth, a time of promises, and a time of dreams. A time of music, a time of drugs, a time of friendships, and a time of life never to be matched.

Hot Rod walked slowly past me, touching my shoulder with a gentle yet firm, lingering squeeze as he walked into my memories through the gray haze. "Hey, Trace. Great to see you," my dear friend called out as he looked back at me with a genuine smile. He sat on the log next to young me, all of sixteen, tall and thin, built for speed (as Joe always said about me), with long, curly auburn hair and wearing a green army jacket, jeans, and high-top white sneakers.

Hot Rod reached over and took the joint. My head exploded into thick white smoke as I exhaled into the air, recalling the line from "Lucy in the Sky with Diamonds" by the Beatles: *Where rocking horse people eat marshmallow pies.*

Slipping her arm more tightly around me, Lori listened to every word as I painted the moment, showing her all the times spent and what they meant to me...to all of us. Joe sang, Mark and Jim talked sports, and Tina and I shot gunned a joint. Like a blur, friends showed up and left, only to show up again. The changing of the seasons passed in a blur, pausing for just a moment at times for very special moments, just as our lives had.

Sweet music always played, and drugs were a part of our daily lives. Love, the pain it caused, as nothing lasts forever, and friendships, bonds that would stand the test of life. *And can you tell me it was worth it?* Stevie asked as the memories continued.

After a moment, my wife started to cry softly in my arms. "This is beautiful, Trace. Thank you." I held her tightly as the memories slowly faded into the past for another time, when maybe another friend would stand here with me and see these memories again.

"Sometimes you will never know the vaule" of something until it becomes a memory ~ Dr. Seuss

"Thanks, babe," I said, "but we have one more stop." We returned to the car, I opened the door for her, and she climbed in. As we slowly came out of the neighborhood, memories flashed through my head. All of fourteen years, I was playing football in the vacant lot next to Oat's house. Young and with long hair, most of us smoked Marlboro cigarettes as we played the game.

Turning left, Lori and I headed for our next stop.

I watched as Tina, and I walked down Green St. toward the beach. Many of us were doing our thirty-minute walk to Bicknell in the morning, and the cars of our time drove by. Steppenwolf's "Magic Carpet Ride" played: *On a cloud of sound,*

I drift in the night. Any place it goes is right. Yes, it did seem Lori and I were on a magic carpet ride back into the seventies of our lives.

After grabbing two cups of hot java from Dunkie's at the corner of Bridge and Green, we drove to the new beach and pulled into the parking lot. As I looked toward the back of the lot where the salt marsh grass grew, I remembered the winter of Sherry. (I still have my twelve-foot Dr. Who scarf she knitted for me. How many nights did we park back there and practice love? Only the most incredible memories of you, my dearest friend.)

Taking off our shoes, Lori and I stepped off the beach wall and onto the sands of my once-upon-a-time. The chatter of a few seagulls filled the air as we walked to the ocean's edge, back again into the summers of my youth.

Hand in hand, my wife and I continued our trek. "All You Need Is Love" by the Beatles floated gently through the air, softly filling the warm summah breeze. *There's nothing you can do that can't be done. (Love, love, love)* Like old black-and-white movies in walking picture frames, the seventies came alive again and danced across the sand.

"Yo, Trace," a voice called from off to my left. At the edge of the beach, just before the hill to the houses above, stood an old friend from years gone by. His straight white hair was parted in the middle and hung down past his shoulders, complemented by a white mustache and long white beard. He wore blue jeans, a blue denim vest with a long silver wallet chain hanging from his waist, and black work boots. He waved a bit, turned, and walked back into the past. If you know this friend, you will not have to ask me who he is. You will find his name in the dictionary under "unique."

"Trace, are you with me?"

I felt a tug on my arm and looked where my old friend had just been.

"No, babe, you are with me."

As Lori and I moved closer to the hard-packed sand at the water's edge, two girls in bikinis walked past us, smoking a joint and laughing.

"Hey, Trace," called fifteen-year-old Jody and Donna, slowing momentarily as they passed the joint between them before continuing their trek down the beach.

So many memories flooded through me as we walked the hard-packed sand. In the distance, I saw a thirteen-year-old boy standing at the water's edge, looking out over the ocean. It was winter, and the Atlantic Ocean was full of anger. "Emma" by Hot Chocolate played sadly on the winter ocean breeze: *But I just can't keep living on dreams no more.*

Next to the teen stood a most faithful companion, a beautiful silver and red Husky. The dog's name was Kara. At the time, the boy had been close to being homeless and alone. He just needed to breathe, and this was where he would come to deal with the loneliness and uncertainty of his life.

A group of teen boys dressed in jeans and flannel shirts walked by as the sun set on a lazy New England summer. They carried two cases of beer, and the smell of pot filled the salty air. How many times did we drink on this beach and get high? For some reason, the cops never made it out to this end of the beach, so it seemed to be a haven as long as it never got too wild.

The past leaped out at me now as the memories flowed like someone shotgunning a can of beer. The beach was full of history: swimming in the cool Atlantic, frisbees and laughter filling the air. The best of times—and the worst—always seemed to happen here. I watched as a young girl yelled at a teen boy, "I don't want to see you anymore!"

Sadly, they never saw each other again, even years later, after a few e-mails. That day was still too fresh in their memories. "I'll Be" by Edwin McCain drifted past, easing the moment of sadness and times gone by and lost: *And I dropped out; I burned up; I fought my way back from the dead.*

I took Lori's hand, and we slowly made our way over the boulders of the jetty to where the ocean met the enormous granite rocks. Sitting at the jetty's edge with the most beautiful woman I had ever known—or would ever know—I thought about how Lori was perfection. Her beautiful, long red hair blew gently across the ivory skin of her beautiful face in the cool summer breeze.

As the warm waves of the Atlantic gently caressed our naked feet, we talked more about growing up. Her life, my life, our life, everyone's life. We talked for hours. I love talking with this woman. During our talk, I stopped for a moment, realizing I had been here thirty years ago to the day.

Lori gave me one of her great smiles and gently nudged me. "Hey, Trace, tell me what you are thinking," this most beautiful woman whispered in my ear.

"I need to finish a story I started here many years ago," I whispered back to the most intense woman I have ever known.

As our lips touched, a line from Fleetwood Mac's "Silver Springs" tumbled through my head: *And can you tell me, was it worth it? Baby, I don't want to know.*

Our story continues ~ trace

Chapter Three

1970

Today was the day my world got bigger.
The reality of it was only a few miles,
But they gave all of us new horizons.
She brought endless possibilities to all of us.
Our world got bigger because we did.
~ trace

"Donny, Donny!"

I pulled off my headphones, and the sweet music of Grand Funk Railroad's *Closer to Home*, my new favorite twelve-inch, thirty-three-RPM album, filled my bedroom. (All these years later, I wonder how my hearing is still good after so many hours in headsets, listening to wicked-loud music.)

I glanced toward the stairs as my mother's yell drowned out the music...almost. "Donny, get down here! Jimmy and Joe are here! You are not spending the summah in the house." As Alice Cooper said: *No more teachers, no more books. School's out forever. School's out for summah.*

I bounced down the stairs and headed out into the morning sunshine. "'Bout time, TRACE." My nickname would last even now, over fifty-plus years later.

"Hey, Joe. Hey, Lung. Just listening to *Closer to Home*." they were my two best friends then, and I am sure, even after all these years of life, that the three of us would never grow tired of each other.

Funny thing about that album, *Closer to Home*. A friend stole it from the record section of W.T. Grant's department store, but he charged me three dollars for it. It was worth every dime. Even today, I know every word to every song on that two-sided, thirty-three-RPM record. I played that album until the groves wore out, and then some.

I'd spent most of my summers for the previous twelve years in my parents' yards or at friends' homes on the local block. Much of the time, I was down at Julia Rd. Park, as every summer, a few park teachers, mainly college students with summer jobs with the town of Weymouth, kept us occupied while our mothers watched television. There was a male park teacher for the boys and a woman for the girls.

The male park teacher put together a baseball team to play against the other parks, while the female park teacher mainly did arts and crafts with the girls. Sadly, yours truly could play baseball, but if you were a few years younger and not very popular, you spent most of the summer sitting on the grass, watching, and hoping for a chance to play that never came.

Yes, every summer vacation, my siblings and I were thrown out of the house for the day by my mother, as the last thing she wanted was a house full of kids. Heck, the last thing my mother wanted was kids. I am pretty sure of that (well, at least me).

During a few of these summers, I did try summer camp at the YMCA, but that was even worse, as it was run by mostly older teens who thought it was fun to abuse the younger ones in their care. I am sure most camp counselors made it acceptable as correctional officers later in life. So, never was I happier when Joe said the words that would change our lives forever.

"We are heading over to Oat's neighborhood to hang out," he said, more as a statement than a request. Yes, we were leaving the safety of our neighborhood to hang out in a foreign one. It could have been Tibet to the three of us, but it was something new. The world was about to get a lot bigger.

It was the summer when the real world started.
Fifty-plus years ago, I was thirteen and a little unsteady as the seventies approached, and I left the safety of Frank Rd. Joe, Jim, and I left our sanctuary of youngness and the sixties and started the long journey of our youth into the seventies and our teens. Drugs, booze, music, sweet music, and girls were just over the horizon.

"I'm game," I said. "Let's go."

The three of us turned up Frank Rd., starting a fifteen-minute journey that would forever change our lives and friendship. After riding across Green St., going down Rinaldo Rd. for a bit, and making a quick turn onto Katherine St., we were in what was to be called then and to this day, some fifty years later, *the neighborhood.*

All through the seventies, whenever we were to hang out or go somewhere, it would always be, "I'll meet you in the neighborhood, and we'll figure it out from there." There never seemed to be a need to set a time to show up there.

If you were bored and didn't want to hang around with your parents at home, you could head to the neighborhood any time, day or night, and other members would show up before you could finish your first cigarette, it seemed. Heck, every night, I worked late at the local pizza joint on Bridge St. Even though it was out of my way, I would take the extra twenty minutes to pass through the neighborhood to hang out before heading home, usually around midnight on a school night. I always told my mother we got busy late so cleaning up took longer. We kids seemed to have to touch the neighborhood every day.

Even now, many years later, on my trips back east from Texas to visit my older brother, Rick, I always make it a point to stop and sit down in the neighborhood and remember the days of my youth.

You were always in the neighborhood. It didn't matter if it was three in the morning; someone would always show up, usually more than just one or two of us. We traveled in packs of three and always met in the neighborhood.

Years later, as we got cars, the neighborhood became a parking lot of three to four vehicles at a time, all blaring different music from radios and eight-tracks simultaneously. The owners of the homes around us never seemed to mind, as their kids were part of the group. In hindsight, that is why the gang stayed tight, as we were never chased away by a phone call to the police or forced to split the street.

Joe, Jim, and I were now in the neighborhood, with three new friends to meet. Yes, life was getting interesting. "Trace, Lung, this is Oats, Shaun, and Tina," Joe announced as we stopped in the middle of the road. The sizing-up had begun, and the moment was upon us as to whether we would be accepted into this new gang or sent back to summah camp at Julia Rd. Park.

The moment seemed to stretch for eternity. Finally, Oats dropped his cigarette to the ground, crushed it out with his shoe, and said the words of acceptance: "Hey, you guys wanna get high?" With that, the newly formed gang of six moved toward the woods just off the street. As Bob Dylan sang: *But I would not feel so all alone. Everybody must get stoned.*

Yes, it was the summer of 1970, between the sixth and seventh grades, and we were entering the world of drugs. Life was about to change, and reefer madness soon welcomed our small but growing gang into its maddening grasp.

Strange. According to the 1936 movie *Reefer Madness*, this melodramatic event was not supposed to happen until high school. Also, according to the movie, we should have been about to commit manslaughter, suicide, and rape while suffering a hallucinatory descent into madness due to this marijuana addiction we were about to embark on.

Years later, Joe, Hot Rod, and I saw this movie at the local drive-in on Morrissey Blvd. in Dorchester. Yes, we were all wicked high and thought the movie deserved an Emmy for its factual depiction of what was happening to us.

In one scene in the movie, a woman is being led down a hall, and she freaks out and jumps to her death, crashing through the window to the street below. At this point, Joe commented, "If there were Frankie's pizza outside, I would have done that. I'm starving. Let's go to the concession stand." But back to the story.

About twenty feet into the woods, a small clearing appeared with a fallen telephone pole on one side. Oats pulled a baggie and a rolled-up cigarette from his front pocket. He handed the cigarette to Shaun.

"Rule number one: he who rolls it gets to spark it," Mark announced to the gang of six.

The ritual was on as Shaun pulled out a blue lighter and held the flame to the end of the joint while inhaling on the other end. The pungent smell hit us quickly as the joint tip turned bright orange from the heat, and the joint crackled as a few seeds popped.

It was as if Shaun had turned to smoke as he exhaled a cloud of white fog so thick you could draw pictures on it, obscuring his head. After a few seconds, he began to snort and cough. "Good stuff," he sputtered as he passed the joint back to Oats, who repeated the process of inhaling and disappearing into the white smoke, followed by coughing.

Tina was next to take the joint. After she took a hit, she said, "Here ya go, Trace," and passed the joint to me. Life was about to change for me as I took the joint from one of my newest forever friends. I didn't even smoke cigarettes, so I had no real idea where this was going or where I would end up.

But yes, I was going. As the smoke filled my lungs, I could feel its warm yet harsh embrace. I held in the smoke for a few seconds, fighting the urge to cough, and Joe called out, "Way to go, Trace!" Finally, I was done, and my head exploded into white smoke. I passed the joint to Lung, who held in the smoke for a wicked-long time.

Lung smiled and passed the joint to Joe as his head exploded. We'd learned over the years of smoking to always pass the joint to Joe last. "Don't bogart that joint, Joe!" was a common refrain, as he tended to take wicked-big hits and almost end the life of the joint in one *Yaz* hit.

They say you never forget your first time, though, in the case of your first high, it'd be perfectly understandable if you did. Nevertheless, the first few hits planted the seed of love for marijuana; we fell in love with weed. Everything about it was perfect: the unquenchable munchies that struck us right after the last hit, the lazy-legs syndrome, the philosophical reflections on the world we shared, and the fact that we couldn't stop laughing at the stupidest things in the room. Our goal was to get as stoned as possible, laugh a lot, quench our munchies, and do whatever was fun while being high.

Over the next few weeks, our neighborhood gang would grow to fourteen kids. We were a diverse group, with sisters, brothers, and single boys and girls, so we also enjoyed day-to-day interactions with the other sex. Lots of dating happened in the group, but it was always easygoing, and I can't remember a lousy break-up over the years. For some reason, yours truly never dated in the gang. Not to say I didn't try, but the girls never saw me as more than a friend. *Yeah, I know, a friend.* Pretty sure some of them never even saw me as that. But hey, we were a gang of fourteen at the time.

We were still trying to figure out how this happened. Some of us heard the calling of a place to hang out. Most of us lived no more than twenty minutes from the sanctuary we called the neighborhood. But when we got to the area, you were away from home and the structure your parents had set up for you. It was a place of music, drugs, and friendship like no other. As I think back on it, I'm reminded of the song "Baba O'Riley" by the Who: *It's only teenage wasteland!*

The neighborhood was where the birth of the seventies occurred for me and many others. Things were changing quickly. Pop culture was being created in the area and across Weymouth. We had made our unique language, which sometimes— okay, always—drove our parents and others of the older generations nuts.

Kinda funny to think there were days when we would stand around for hours and talk, laugh, and hate to go home. We would meet there after school and plan our evenings or weekends and always go from there. There was always a joint, and soon Bud and whiskey to drink. Some of the gang had older siblings who would hit up the packie for us just to shut us up for a hefty price.

The gang maxed out at fifteen. Most times, we were all there in the neighborhood. Sometimes three or four of us would head off to some far-flung place, but we'd always return a few hours later. We never traveled outside our little spot en masse, only in small groups, and we'd always return with our stories of valor and humor to share with the gang. Heck, some of the stories were even true.

It is essential to mention here why Weymouth is the birthplace of the seventies. There were at least ten other gangs in the small town, and all were incredibly unique in their own way, but the love of music and drugs was universal. We all knew each other, mainly from high school and when we went to the Esker parties at night, but we rarely dropped into another gang's space unless we were on the hunt for drugs.

Now, many folks would enter the neighborhood over the years. Some would stay a few months, and others just a few days. Some were there for just a few hours. Except one.

When did this person arrive? Maybe early to mid-seventies. He tagged along with another person into the neighborhood one day. When the other person left, this kid stayed, as he *liked our style*. He quickly became an enduring member of the neighborhood gang, making it complete in many ways. His name was Richard Smith, but we called him Hot Rod. From day one, we all loved him. Our gang was now complete at fifteen.

With a friend at hand, you will see the light
If your friends are there then everything's all right
~ Elton John, "Friends"

Our story continues ~ trace

Chapter Four

Around the Log

Time to hide.
Time to just run away.
I am not ready for your life.
I am now ready to begin mine.
Your big band is not my rock band.
Short hair versus long hair, it is my hair.
I am not really lazy; I am exploring my mind.
I see the years ahead, but they are ahead of me.
I see today for what it is, what it could be, should be.
I see your wisdom of age, feel and see my pain of youth.
Things have really changed; a revolution is now finally at hand.
A revolution is not planned; the '70s are here change is happening.
~ trace, 1972

I can't begin to tell you how many hours the gang, in varying numbers, would sit around for hours and talk about the most ridiculous things while getting high. (We never ran out of pot.) We all had our *something* that each of us brought to the group. We all brought music as our thing, but Joe brought music as his *schtick*. Oats and James brought sports as their *schtick*. I never really brought much in the way of knowledge, but I always enjoyed all the *schticks* in the group. (Even now, I am a better listener than a talker.) Tina brought friendship, music, weed, and a deep understanding of life as her *schtick*. Hot Rod brought (you guessed it) an understanding of cars as his *schtick*. It seemed most of the gang had some *schtick,* but we all had a love for drugs, music, and friendships in common, which bonded us more than we would ever know, even years later.

By eleven, smoking herb and drinking burning liquor.
~ Lukas Graham, "7 Years"

Kids would drop into the neighborhood from other parts of Weymouth to score weed or see what was happening in our world. We all had wanderlust. Some would stay the night. Others would stroll in and out of the neighborhood, bringing their *schtick*. When we were high, there was always cause for lively debate, and topics ranged from cars that ran on water, which the gas companies kept off the market, to just about anything the government was doing in secret. Mainly, though, we talked about UFOs that had crashed on Earth.

The only *schtick* I never really had much use for was *I know everything*. This one tended to cause a few problems, especially when people were drunk. The gang was lucky we never really had a full-time *I know everything* member, so most of our mindless chatter left us laughing until tears ran down our cheeks.

So many moments of us around the log over the years run through my mind as I listen to BTO's "Taking Care of Business": *If it were easy as fishin', you could be a musician.* Here are just a few.

"Trace, take a hit," Jim called out as Tina passed the joint over to me. Her eyes watered as she tried to hold the harsh smoke in as long as she could. Rule number two: the longer the hold, the better the high. (Or so the story goes.)

Joe, Oats, Tina, Jim, and yours truly were having a typical day down in the neighborhood, smoking lots of weed. It never mattered how low you were. Weed would take you to a high of hope, dreams, music, great thoughts, and, of course, munchies.

"I can't believe Fisk tore up his knee yesterday," Jim said to no one in particular. He was referring to the Boston Red Sox star catcher who tore up his knee while blocking the plate in a game against the Cleveland Indians.

"The Sox still have El Tiant and the Spaceman," Joe said, taking the joint from me as Tina exploded in a coughing fit. The smoke had finally gotten the better of her. Grabbing my shoulders for support, she caught her breath and took a long swing of the Bud Jim handed her to help chase away the coughing.

"Doesn't matter what the Sox do," said Oats, taking the joint from Joe. "The A's are winning it all this year." Now it was my turn to break out coughing from the harsh smoke, and Tina passed me the beer.

"You're nuts, Oats," said Jim as Oats passed the joint over to him. "The Sox are kicking ass this year." As if on cue, Joe let out a ragged cough as he exhaled a cloud of thick gray smoke. I passed the beer to him.

"We talk about the Sox every day," said Tina. She didn't like it when we talked about sports, but when it came to music, this pretty friend of mine could hold her own with the best of us.

"Yeah, let's talk about the B's for a bit," Jim said, winking at Tina. He took a resounding hit on the joint, and the tip glowed brightly in the early sunset. Passing the joint to Tina, he smiled as some smoke seeped out of his lips. He leaned back, starting to feel high. Heck, we were all baked.

"Come on, Trace," said Tina. "Shotgun." She blew the smoke from her lungs into my waiting open mouth. Our lips were not quite touching, but all the smoke made it safely from her to me. I bet she and I did a few thousand shotguns over the years. I cherish our friendship even today, fifty years later.

Joe started singing "It's Only Rock 'n' Roll (But I Like It)" by the Rolling Stones. After a moment, we all joined in as the joint made its rounds once again.

Sometimes, memories of the log will crash down on me all at once. It was our meeting place, but really, it was where we went to smoke the *boo,* as Joe and I called pot, where no one could see us. The name never really caught on, but it worked for us. Only six of us could fit on the log at one time.

Most meetings started *and continued* with the lighting of a joint. Depending on the mix of the gang at the time, topics covered girls we liked, music (always), sports, school, and the next joint. All of us were great students in school and valued our educations, but for some reason, I never once heard someone say, "I need to go do my homework." Despite this, most of the gang moved forward through school and had plans for their futures.

To the young folks reading about your parents (or grandparents) growing up in the seventies, not having cell phones was the first and most crucial hardship. *WHAT?* Yes, it's true. If we needed information, we sent scouts to find out what was happening. If we needed to talk to a friend, we would go to their house or would meet up somewhere in the neighborhood and figure it out there.

The second major problem was getting pot. You gotta remember, weed was illegal everywhere in the country. It was considered a gateway drug to harder drugs like heroin. Beats me as to why that was. Smoking weed did reduce short-term memory, reduced motivation, and led to nonstop laughing and the munchies, to name just a few things this bit of Mother Nature did to all of us.

The War on Drugs started in 1970. (I guess the government knew we had started smoking in the neighborhood). This "war" was, in fact, a government-led initiative to stop illegal drug use, distribution, and trade by dramatically increasing prison sentences for both drug dealers and users. In Massachusetts during the seventies, using or dealing could land you in jail for two to fifteen years and lead to a fine of up to twenty-five thousand dollars.

As far as I know, no one from the gang ever got locked up for holding or dealing pot, but because of this law, it was always a good idea to run if the police approached when you had pot on you, dumping your stash where you could pick it up later if you got caught. The few times anyone got caught with pot in their possession, the police dumped it into the ground and told them to go home, with a *next time you might not be so lucky* warning or threat, depending on the cop.

Now, when I think back to the days we hung out in the neighborhood, they seem to blend into each other. Oh, sure, small things happened daily, but not really. Each day was more of the same but on a different day. Depending on the time of year, the gang might not show up till after school. On weekends and summers, the gang would hear the call to meet around noon, make plans for the night, and head home for dinner or check in with family around four. Afterward, we'd shower, change clothes, and return to the neighborhood.

Depending on Joe's music schedule, I usually met up with Mark, and we'd head out to where Joe and the band were playing that night. Others in the group never really followed Joe's tour (as I always called it) but would head off to other places for the night or hang in the 'hood and head for the skies in a starship made of smoke.

Rarely would we all be in the neighborhood simultaneously, as the gang still had social and family commitments, but we would all be there at some point during the day and night. It often seemed like we were taking shifts. At times, we showed up in groups of three or four and left with others. Some would stay as the next group appeared and then head out on some adventure. We always returned to the neighborhood before heading home to get filled in on what was happening around Weymouth, learning where we could get some food, what new tune everyone was listening to, or where the best pot was.

Right now, I'm listening to "Woke Up This Morning" by the Alabama 3. The beat perfectly expresses the nights of music, highs, dreams, and fears. *'Cause when you woke up this morning, everything you had was gone.*

Our story continues ~ trace

Chapter Five

Friendships

"Truly great friends are hard to find, difficult to leave, and impossible to forget." ~ *Anonymous*

For all the attention we pay to the stories we love, some of the most compelling tales (both fiction and not) are those of very best friends, like Thelma and Louise, Woody and Buzz, and even Captain Kirk and Spock. These friends had each other's backs through thick and thin despite the many bumps in the road along the way. But much like romance, if you've ever tried to make a new friend and things didn't click, it's likely because one of the essential components of friendship wasn't there. Did we all click in the neighborhood? I doubt it, but it did seem we all liked each other (some more than others.) Here are a few stories that show just how special these friendships were.

One Moment Out of Many with Tina

"Hey, Trace, do me a favor and walk Tina home for me again," Scott called from across the street as he walked out of the woods with Tina in tow. This had become a daily thing over the last few months. Around six or so, Tina needed to start the trek to her home near the North Weymouth Library. Somehow, this had become my job and not her boyfriend's. Heck, I didn't mind. It was Tina, the prettiest, sweetest, and just plain hottest girl in Weymouth. Five-foot-nothing, with long, curly hair, she had a smile that could launch a thousand ships and a wink that set the world on fire.

"Sure, Scott, no problem," I called back, and then Tina and I started our walk-up Green Street. Over the last few weeks, she and I had been filling our walks with talk about life, music, and everything a couple of kids in their early teens could think of. And what the heck, we just enjoyed each other. We were, and are, best buds.

Our walk led us to Shaw Street, where we would usually take a left for the final half-mile to Tina's home, but today, we just kept walking for the next half-hour until we hit the new beach, chatting away to each other the whole time.

"Hey, Trace, we missed our turn," Tina said. We both started laughing when we realized we had missed it about two miles back. There was no one else on the beach.

"That's fine," I said. "Let's head down to the old beach and take North Street to your house."

As if she already knew that would be the plan, Tina was about five steps ahead of me, heading for the hard sand where the ocean lapped onto the beach.

We took our shoes off and continued our conversation about life, Scott, Joe, Lung, Oats, the gang, and everyone we could think of in school while we strolled down the new beach to the old one.

Now, anyone who has ever made this walk knows that a massive rock jetty splits the beaches. This is where Tina decided it was time to stop for a rest. "Trace let's stop here for a bit," she said and then climbed to the top of the jetty and sat down.

"No problem, T. Dinner can wait," I replied as I sat next to her.

The summer sun was beginning to set. Anyone who has sat on one of these jetties knows the beauty of the ocean when it is calm or angry, and enjoyed the picturesque scenes of the boats at anchor or floating lazily over the smooth, glass-like sea of the Atlantic.

The smell of pot slowly engulfed me. Ahh, that smell. Turning around toward Tina, I watched as she tilted her head back and slowly blew the harsh, sweet smoke into the cool evening air.

"Shotgun, Trace," she whispered as she coughed a bit from the harsh smoke. Turning the joint around, she put the lit end in her mouth, and we moved close to each other. Our lips barely scraped, held apart only by the smoke and the end of the joint.

For some reason, pot always tasted better when I shot-gunned it with Tina.

Mr. J.W. (Joe)

Whaddaya say about this man? I grew up and shared some of my best and all of my worst times with this friend. I would call him my best friend, but that wouldn't be fair to many who considered him theirs, so I will gladly call him a friend I love very much.

Nothing describes our friendship better than what has been written here. I smile every time a special moment from our youth drifts slowly to the surface of my memories. I'm walking down Katherine Street, at the edge of the neighborhood, and see a yellow Chrysler as big as a whale, large enough to seat twenty, parked under the light pole across from Oat's house.

The evening has been around for hours, but the darkness is held back by the lone streetlight hanging from the top of the pole. Two kids are leaning against the driver's side of the car, smoking a joint. One passes the joint to the other. When I got closer, I recognize one of the kids: Joe.

"Here ya go, Trace," Joe says, passing the joint to a waiting hand. As I take the joint, I realize the other kid is me. I inhale deeply, and the smoke brings that crazy haze we have come to love.

Then Joe does what he does best, what he always was and always will be meant to do. He begins to sing. Not just any song but one we would cherish and sing at the weirdest times over the years. The song is "Lonely Boy" by Andrew Gold.

Pausing momentarily, Joe plucks the joint from my fingers and takes a J.W. hit (way too much). After handing the joint back to me, in typical Joe fashion, he looks at me and says, "Come on, Trace, we got this!"

He was born on a summer day in 1951.

We begin to sing together, as if the world is listening and cheering us on. But all that's listening are the memories being made.

I smile a bit as I watch this memory of the rock star and his friend, singing under the lights of our youth, as it slowly fades away under the streetlight.

When I tell people about our friendship, I say, "My oldest friend is Music. I call him Joe."

"What I learned about memories is that they hold a moment that's gone forever, impossible to reproduce." ~ trace

I have learned not to try to hold on to these memories as they fade. I know they will be back. The rock star and his friend are memories I will treasure all my life. It is one of the blessings of friends that you can afford to be stupid with them and not be held accountable.

As you go through this book of memories, you will see that much of it is about Joe, Jim, Tina, Mark, and me. I am guessing it's because we were always each other's first call when it came to finding something to do. I can't count the number of times we smoked pot one on one or in small groups, or the places we ended up. So many times, we found ourselves far from home, like on another planet, toasted to the max or tripping our brains out. The two of us always had wandering spirits, racing like two crazy wooden ships on a poster hung on the wall of life.

I remember standing in the middle of Mattapan Square, smoking a joint with a few locals at two in the morning. We'd taken the wrong bus from downtown Boston after leaving one of the watering holes we had been in that night. This was during Joe's B.C. High days, which brought us new places and people to party with...and party we did

.

Memories of Joe's music will forever be intertwined with our friendship.

Skip

"Trace, if it was you, me, and Skip, trust me, it could only be about DRUGS, BOOZE, and MUSIC. Period. Nothing else." ~ J.W.

One of the most unique people I've ever met, not just in my youth but to this day, well over fifty years later, was Mr. Skip Tuttle. Skip left too early in life, in May of 2010. He could do any substance quicker, longer, and faster than anyone I have ever known. (Also, to this day, Skip is the only man who has ever kissed me. But that is another story for another time.)

Joe, Skip, and I had just spent the last two hours at Axis practice at a band member's house on the South Shore. (Axis was a band Joe and Skip were in at the time.) We'd smoked a ton of weed during practice. Afterward, we drove down to one of the many Hingham beaches and walked down the beach, still smoking up a storm.

Spending time with Joe and Skip was like being with a couple of jukeboxes—music, sweet music, and air guitars blazing. In a stoned haze, we sang the Tubes song "TV Is King." After about an hour of this, Skip thought Chinese food was the next best thing to music. The closest place to eat was right down the street, just a few miles away. Off we went; pupu platters, Dr. Funks, scorpion bowls, and so much more weed were on the menu.

The second the three of us walked through the restaurant doors, Skip decided he was Chinese. "Table three, please," he said in perfect Chinese broken English, squinting his eyes in the dim light.

`For some reason, the staff thought putting us three at a half-round booth was a good idea, so we all sat together, with Joe on one side, Skip in the middle, and yours truly on the other side of Skip. You must remember, back in the seventies, there was no such thing as too much to drink at a restaurant, and we proved it on this night.

"May I get you something to drink?" the server asked as she approached the half-moon booth, as Joe called it. Before Joe or I could answer, Skip said in his perfect Chinese broken English, "We have three Doctor Funks, six Bud bottles, two pupu platters, beef lo mien, fried lice, and steamed lo mien." Then he waved the server away with a "Now, please." We were on our way.

The Doctor Funks were quickly downed and replaced by scorpion bowls, two times three. The Buds went just as quickly, followed by six Haffenreffers—green deaths, as Joe loved to call them, due to their green bottles. A waiter would come by every few minutes and say, "No smoking weed in the restaurant." We assured them they were just rolled cigarettes, but we stopped after a few hits.

We were about thirty minutes into our Roman banquet when it got even more fun, or was it the finale, as the smiling people of the restaurant asked us to leave a few minutes later? Skip had decided we would do 151 Bacardi rum shots. That was no reason to throw up, but how we did the shots was. Skip loved to push the limits when it came to drinking, drugging, and music, and he thought we could hit those limits with all three in rapid succession.

Skip ordered three shots of the contaminated liquid for each of us. After they were lined up on the table, there would be a slam-it-down race to determine who could knock back their three shots first. (What were we thinking? Oh, right. We weren't thinking.)

"GO!" Skip shouted.

Boom! I grabbed the first shot from the table and tossed it back. As my eyes watered, I started to gag but somehow got it down. My head was on fire. Looking over, I saw Joe was not doing any better but was beginning his second shot. Skip, the trooper, was already headed for his third. I grabbed my second shot and threw the nasty, burning liquid down my throat.

Bam! Skip threw up on the table; the third shot had been too much. A river of Chinese food and Dr. Funks ran everywhere. I started to gag. Lifting the tablecloth, I emptied my food and drinks onto the floor under the table. Joe threw up next to Skip. Unable to make it under the table, he put most of his food and drink in the aisle.

After a few minutes of throwing up, Skip asked for fortune cookies.

My dearest Skip, you are missed and will always be loved by me and many others.
Until we meet again, party hard and well.

Jimmy

James moved in a few streets over in the late sixties, and our friendship was immediate. We always seemed to be the first to start the daily trek down to the neighborhood, as we were the farthest away, and we would stop and get Joe on our way. It was the same but in reverse going home. Jim, Joe, and I were inseparable growing up. In many ways, they were my only true family.

Jim and I would head up to Jackson Square, at the corner of Middle and Broad Streets, a few times a month to get pizza and look for chicks. You know, the pizza place up by the old Y; there used to be a bike shop across from it. I got my first bike there years ago. We would get a large cheese pizza and two Cokes, sit down, and watch all the girls come in. For some reason, this was a hot spot for girls our age on the weekends. We would talk loudly to get noticed, discussing drugs, music, and drinking down in the neighborhood. I never got a date. I can't understand why...

I loved Jim's parents like they were my own, and I would spend hours talking with them if I had a problem that needed an adult's perspective. They were the parents I never had. Thank you, Jim, for allowing our friendship and your parents to be a part of my life.

I can't remember a day in our youth when Jim and I weren't together. We were on the same sports teams, we always walked together to school, and we tended to leave the neighborhood together, as we lived close to each other.

Jim and I were always game to go anywhere. Heck, we walked to the old Grossman's in Braintree one day to see the tank they had behind the wall and then walked back home and played a street hockey game against the Doughboys that day. We ran across Whitman's Pond one winter just ahead of the cracking ice, racing from the roller-skating rink to the other side by the projects to see if we could. As we ran, we sank in the slush past our ankles once or twice and had to stop to put our shoes back on after they'd gotten pulled off. Somehow, we made it and didn't fall in and drown. Years later, I lost a friend one summer on that pond while drinking and partying.

I talked with Jim when I returned to the Cape a few months ago to see him and Joe. We spent the night laughing and saying nothing until Joe's wife chased us out in the early morning hours. Jim and I laughed for a few more minutes in Joe's drive-way. After we hugged each other, we climbed into our cars and drove slowly away.

A few weeks ago, I called Jim to tell him I would be in Boston soon and wanted to give him a copy of the book about our youth. We talked briefly, and he had many memories to share. He reminded me of how we made tacos in my mom's kitchen. When it came to Jim and Joe being in the house, it was always okay with my parents, and they never needed to knock or leave.

I told him that I had left a lot unsaid the last time we were at Joe's. This bothered me greatly because I had so much to say to one of the best friends I have known, or ever will know. I hadn't been there for some rough moments in his life years ago. For many years, I never admitted how scared I'd been to step in and be a true friend. (This failure has haunted and shamed me for many years.) He told me he understood, to not worry about it, and forgave me.

Love you, Jim. You are my brother.

Oats

My friendship with Mark, or Oats, was, to say the least, wild. I went to my first strip bar with him in the famed Combat Zone in Boston when life was legal for eighteen-year-olds. We went to the Naked Eye and spent every dime we had in, like, ten minutes. But we did see some stunning women take their clothes off. Worth every cent we spent over the years in this famed nightspot.

We'd go to the dog track and make two-dollar wages. I saw it as fun and a place to drink. Not Mark; he went to win each race. Sadly, he never won more than he lost, but it was always a close race. I can't count how many races we spent money on at the dog track. For some reason, we never saw a horse race.

We also spent hours driving around in his yellow two-door Camaro to find the best pot. Most weekends, we drove all over the South Shore, getting stupidly high and chasing down the latest club where Joe would be playing in one of the many bands he was a part of over the years. Mark never once asked for gas money from anyone.

Oats was the traveling man in our gang. Over the years, he was known as the commissioner in our strat leagues. Mark was easygoing and quick with a laugh or comeback, and even today, I consider him one of my closest friends.

Mark, my man, so many miles we traveled together when we were young. So many laughs, so many highs, so many Buds. When our days come, let's travel more miles together to a new space, a new time.

Nick "The Man" Rello

Gee, what can you say about this man? Nick was a few years older than me and, to my mind, the toughest kid in Weymouth. I passed him often in school hallways, but we didn't run in the same gang, so we never talked. If there was trouble in school, Nick was in it. He ran with the team up in the square. They hung out at Beal's Park off Athens Street and called themselves the Beal's Park Gang. If you felt the need to get into a fight, this was the place where you would find it. Thankfully, I never felt the need to get beaten up.

I met Nick formally at his after-wedding party at his parents' house, down by the beach near North Street. The party was outside, and four of us from the neighborhood wandered into the yard. I wasn't sure we were welcome, but I was about to find out as Nick walked up to me in a powder-blue tux with a beer in his hand. "Welcome to my home," he said, holding out his hand. "You're Trace, right?"

Relieved that I wasn't about to get punched in the face, I took his hand, and we shook. "Yes, Nick, I am, and thank you for allowing me to join your party. Congratulations on your marriage."

"Not at all. It is good to meet you finally. Have a beer, and let's get high later." He laughed, and then his wife came over and dragged him away to meet another guest.

Over the years, I would bump into Nick in the strangest places, and high we would get. He always had the time to come over and shake my hand. I spent many a night getting high and drunk with this man, drinking cold beers, smoking a fatty, and just talking about life. Nick left us in January 2012.

Nick, I don't think many folks knew of our friendship or how often we chatted and got high. I look forward to the day when we can talk for hours again. Until we meet again.

Richard (Hot Rod) Smith

At the beginning of this book, I introduced Richard as the friend who completed our gang. Among friends, he was known as Hot Rod or Dick, but I usually referred to him as Dick when we were around strangers or new people in the neighborhood.

I was always willing to go wherever Dick suggested, whether it was The Combat Zone, the Weymouth Fair, or any place to have a good time and drink.

Richard and his parents were incredibly kind, and I had the privilege of meeting them multiple times throughout the years. Unfortunately, Richard passed away too soon from cancer. This kid was truly genuine in every way. Hot Rod will forever remain a cherished member of The Neighborhood Gang.

Rick I am proud to have known you and glad you called me friend. I wish we had more time to chat late into the night. Till we meet again you made our gang so complete in so many ways.

The neighborhood gang was made up of fifteen friends, held together by common bonds of friendship and belonging to something new. The seventies were something special, from clothes to music and drugs. I could write pages about each person in the gang, but this book can only be so long. Some had a more significant impact on my life than others. Some didn't care about me or my life. Heck, some didn't even like me. That's okay, though, as I am pretty sure that went both ways.

The sad part is that so many of us died over the years of our youth. Our time in the seventies was filled with losing friends to drugs, drinking, and partying wickedly. Many of us thought we were indestructible and would live forever. Some of us just wanted to make it through another day but couldn't.

Ooh, a storm is threatening
My very life today.
If I don't get some shelter,
Ooh, yeah, I'm gonna fade away.

~ Rolling Stones, "Gimmie Shelter"

Our story continues ~ trace

Chapter Six

Music Sweet Music

I was talking with Joe and James the last time my travels brought me back to the neighborhood. I was home in Weymouth from the great state of Tex-ass. Age had caught up with us, but we talked late into the night, remembering the amazing times we'd had with music. Our generation had been on the front line of two or three music revolutions, but now all we have are these memories.

I feel the sadness of our time gone by.
The days have piled up in and endless flow of kids, bills, and life.
The seasons come and go, the moons wax and wane,
and sixty-plus years have now flown by in the blink of an eye.
How long will I remember the years of our youth...our music...?
Till the day I die.
~ trace

Both hard rock and soft carved out places in the music world in the 1970s. Some of the best rock 'n' roll of all time was recorded in the seventies, the years of my youth. This most amazing music wasn't just born in this decade—it was a way of life! Our era was much like a "members only" club. How could one possibly describe what it was like to anyone who wasn't there? But we were there...oh, we were there.

Music defined each and every one of us. *We were the music we listened to.* We dressed as the bands of the seventies and quoted lyrics from our favorite songs in deep, pot-fueled conversations about life and meaning. Our music determined our personalities in so many ways. *Heck, I even went through a Harry Chaplain phase. Just a sad loner, always outside the lights and world. Still am in so many ways, even today.*

Hard rock ~ *Weymouth's first choice* started in the 1970s and quickly emerged as the most prominent subgenre of rock music. During the first half of the decade, British acts such as Deep Purple, Led Zeppelin, Uriah Heep, and Black Sabbath were at the height of their international fame, particularly in Weymouth. By the second half of the decade, many other acts had also achieved stardom: Aerosmith, Grand Funk Railroad, Alice Cooper, AC/DC, Cooper, Blue Öyster Cult, Kiss, Van Halen, and Ted Nugent, to name a few. These hard rock bands dominated in Weymouth.

Arena rock ~*Weymouth's second choice* grew in popularity through acts such as Boston, Kansas, Styx, Journey, Toto, Foreigner, and Heart. Most of these bands followed me into my lost years and through the eighties. *But like I said, the lost years are for another time.*

Progressive rock ~ *Weymouth's third choice*, the American brand of progressive rock, varied from the eclectic and truly innovative Frank Zappa, Blood, Sweat & Tears, and Rush to more pop-rock-oriented bands like Boston, Foreigner, Journey, Kansas, and Styx.

Bluegrass music ~ I would be remiss if I didn't mention bands such as the Outlaws, Pure Prairie League, and the

Grateful Dead, whose music filled out the days of a small but dedicated group of friends. *Check out "Three Songs for a Quarter" for a few funny moments about bluegrass.*

The arm of the record player slowly lowered, followed by the scratch of the needle on the record. After a few moments: *BA-DA-DA-DAAAA! Hey, well, I'm the friendly stranger in the black sedan. Woncha hop inside my car?* The year was 1970, and life for me was about to change as I was now in the sixth grade. The song was "Vehicle" by The Ides of March, outta the windy city called Chicago. It was in the sixth grade that I gained my first real understanding of music, thanks to Mr. Anderson.

"My broken spirit is frozen to the core. I don't wanna be here no more."
~ Nik Kershaw, "Wouldn't It Be Good"

Mr. Anderson had brought some records and started music appreciation for an hour a few times over the week. Around the end of the day, he would just have us listen to the music, and then the class would discuss the song. Sometimes, we would all just sing along with the record. Simon & Garfunkel, the Association, the Beatles, Grass Roots, Ides of March, and the Kinks filled our afternoons with songs like "Wendy," "Along Came Mary," "Vehicle," "Why Don't You Write Me," "and Lola. *Remember how mad Mr. Anderson got when we yelled out a certain part of this song?* Our music appreciation hour, as we liked to call it, would change our musical lives. Thank you, Mr. Anderson, for teaching us to express ourselves through our music.

A new way to listen to tunes came along in the early seventies. It didn't need to be plugged in or set on a sturdy structure to avoid skipping. Rain or shine, hot or cold, you could now listen to your favorite songs anytime, anywhere. No high-tech, high-expense, high-profile audio system today could ever capture the rich sounds that came out of my Philips AM/FM transistor radio with a silver faceplate and black case with a handle and six D batteries. The great sounds that came from the radio had nothing to do with the engineering moxie of the audio company, but rather, what came out of it: passionate, livewire, one-of-a-kind disc jockeys playing music that sounded great.

The first real green deal and effort to save the planet happened when Crosby, Stills, Nash & Young took us to Yasgur's farm, where we *"Got to get back to the land. Set my soul free."* The journey to Woodstock was alive on our radios, and we could always take a trip. *And we've got to get ourselves back to the garden.* John Lennon asked us to *"Imagine there's no Heaven. It's easy if you try. No Hell below us. Above us, only sky.*

Music became our news. The music was fun, and the disc jockeys made it that much more fun. It sounded like most announcers were having a great time rather than fitting into a generic, it-sounds-the-same-in-every-city radio show.

The beat didn't stop there in our music growth. WRKO-AM 680 outta Boston jammed twenty-four seven. There was always the promise of non-stop music right after the news, kinda like at the carnival rides at Paragon Park. "Come on back for a really fast ride next time!" the kid operating the ride yelled out as we ran to get back in the hour-long line. *Grin*

As Harry Chapin said in 1973, "Remember how we listened to the radio? And I said, 'That's the place to be.'" Yes, music was the place to be. To this day, so many days later, music is still the place to be.

Harry Nelson, WRKO ~ Phenomenal radio talent—in my opinion, the very best disc jockey to ever spin vinyl over the radio. Nelson had an intense, rapid-fire way of speaking, as if he hadn't been to the bathroom in a month. As one of the most identifiable personalities on the station, he also helped create the WRKO sound.

Harry Nelson was known in every elementary and junior high school playground for his glib, almost out-of-control personality. Many parents knew him as a pusher of music they just didn't understand. We knew better; Nelson was one of our radio idols, simply an amazing radio personality.

Arnie "Woo Woo" Ginsburg ~ Arnie may have been the greatest and most successful talent ever to grace Boston airwaves. He was known for his collection of bells, whistles, horns, and other sound effects, which he frequently used on air during his show. He was often called "Woo-Woo" because of the train whistle he used as part of that collection of sound effects.

It's the summer of '73 in the neighborhood and New England. The gang is huddled around the portable radio sitting on the log. Each of us waits for our favorite song to play so we can show off our musical knowledge.

The Midnight Special ~ This American late-night musical variety series premiered in August 1972. The ninety-minute program aired on Saturday mornings at 1 a.m. I experienced my first Aerosmith and AC/DC concerts by watching this late-night show. By the end of its tenure, I must have watched over a hundred different bands, all while high. Just ask Wolfman Jack.

Don Kirshner's Rock Concert ~ This show was noted for featuring live recorded performances, unusual for the period since most television appearances at that time consisted of lip-synching to prerecorded music. BTO was *Taking Care of Business*. Cheap Trick showed up *At Budokan*. Grand Funk Railroad introduced themselves as *An American Band*. Foghat took us on a *Slow Ride.* Don Kirshner's show was the ultimate rock and roll program of an incredible era in music.

Saturday Night Live ~ Without a doubt, at least to me, this was the late-night show of shows for a generation striving to be new and bold.

The show featured Chevy Chase, John Belushi, Dan Aykroyd, Gilda Radner, Garrett Morris, Jane Curtin, and Laraine Newman.

I think most of us would agree the first cast was the best. They took us to a whole new view of life and laughter. I still remember heading home, turning the television to Channel Four —high as a kite most times—and quietly laughing for ninety minutes. As funny as the show was, the guest band would always play twice during the show. In their first appearance of the night, the band always played something new. The second tune was always an older one, usually a classic.

MTV ~ The greatest musical channel of all-time hit our televisions on August 1, 1981. Now, the seventies have passed, but the importance of this new music delivery system can never be understated. Our music hit the airwaves with a walk and a style that just screamed the seventies, cementing its place of importance for the ages, not just to listen to but to view...to dream.

Matchbox Twenty's "Don't Get Me Wrong" plays quietly into the night as I remember the music of my younger years and how it defined who I was at the time. "I'm a strong man, weaker than I once was. Weed and bramble, still hard to handle."

Is it just me, or does music truly define who we are? These lyrics softly wail the song of my life, as I have grown in so many ways over these many years: "I'm flying blind, but I can see you."

One of the more important aspects in our quest for music in Weymouth and around the country cost us only sixty-five cents. I still remember climbing aboard the T bus at Bicknell Square and paying fifteen cents for the twenty-minute ride to Quincy Center. After getting off the bus at the Quincy Center Post Office, I always had time for a stop at Wooden Ships to check out the latest wall posters and drug paraphernalia (*I never owned a bong*), Colman's Sports, where layaways were accepted, for my latest hockey equipment, and Napoli Pizza for a slice and a Coke. Most of my trips to the center, however, were about music.

I'm not sure of its name anymore, but in the center was a record store. Usually by myself, I'd spend around an hour each visit going through all the forty-five records, trying to find the perfect mix of music. You needed to flip the record over to find what song was on the other side. Depending on the point system in your head, the forty-five would provide at least three days of non-stop music back home—my place most of the time. For some reason, being homeless never allowed for a record player.

The forty-five was the preferred delivery mechanism for rock music, something that cannot be overstated. It was the format favored by pop music radio, jukebox manufacturers and operators, and, for a time, record shops. Sales of forty-fives peaked in 1974, when more than two hundred million vinyl discs were sold. When you played them, you always had to remember to use the all-important yellow plastic adapter.

In our quest for the perfect blends of rich rock tunes, it seemed there was always something else to try: bigger speakers, better stereo setups, and more effective ways of cleaning each piece of vinyl for the deep, rich sound we all craved. It was never enough. No matter what we tried, it always seemed like there was more we could do.

One cold winter day, Joe and I headed over to Butch's home off Bridge Street. When we got there, we found his room covered in tinfoil: the walls, ceiling, windows, even the inside of his door.

"Wadda ya think?" Butch said as he handed Joe an unlit joint and a lighter.

"I don't know," said Joe. "Let's hear it." After lighting the joint, he took a deep hit and passed it back to Butch. A moment later, Butch passed the joint to me.

As I took my hit, the man of tin coughed out a cloud of smoke and said, "Ya gonna love this." Then he went to the turntable and hit the play button.

We listened to the *click-click* of the tone arm lifting and then watched it make its slow descent toward the spinning 33-rpm vinyl. After a few revolutions of the record, a whole new way of listening to music came our way, *BOOM*, off the wall and right back at us, wave after wave of music: *This is a thing I've never known before. It's called easy livin'.* The music filled the room, saturating the three of us with music.

The joint quickly caught up with the music assault, as Uriah Heep never left the air and continued to grow until we were consumed by a non-stop tin room of easy livin'.

A few weeks later, Joe and I walked into another tin room. High as kites, we strolled down Green Street and crossed over Bridge Street onto Neck Street. As most of us know, we were heading in the general direction of the new beach. Close to the beach, we headed up—*I think*—Bradmere Way to Phil's house. We entered through the garage, down into a small, finished basement covered in tin.

The place was already jumping, with about ten teens sitting against the walls and passing a bong around the room. "Hey, Joe, Trace, have a seat and get high!" Phil called out, and we took a seat on a couch near the entrance. The bong made it to us after a moment, and the warm haze settled over us quickly.

It's funny...I can't remember the music that was playing, but I know we were wicked high in that room covered in tin. Seems appropriate that the only song I can think of right now had not yet been released, but what the heck? As Jon Pousette-Dart would say, *"I hope that it's only amnesia. Believe me, I'm sick but not insane."*

The music of the seventies was pure *wow*, a combination of poetic songwriting, experimental, cutting-edge instruments, totally wild costumes, thrilling stage performances, and laser shows. Record companies back in the seventies were more open to supporting up-and-coming artists.

Most of the stories about our lives are laced with music. Like hypnotism, the songs of our youth bring back the moment. For me, at least, music is truly the fastest and most effective way to go back in time. Rock 'n' roll tunes, no matter what your preference, never fail to make us feel something, may it be longing, sadness, aching, happiness, memories, or even pain.

As Bowling for Soup says, *"When did Motley Crue become classic rock? And when did Ozzy become an actor?"*

The seventies were a crucial period in the history of pop and rock music, when musical genres were redefined, new styles were explored, and musicians from various parts of the world experimented with different sounds. Such artistic endeavors left behind a rich legacy that continues to inspire modern-day musicians. Hopefully, they will continue to do so far into the future. *I want my great-grandchildren to experience the music of the seventies.*

Music saved my life, both emotionally and physically, during my homeless times and lost years. In many ways, music was a friend during the bad times of my life. No matter how far down you go, there's always a song to get you back to where you can live. Sometimes, that song stays with you for months, keeping the promise of salvation in time.

I will leave you with my top-ten bands of the seventies: Aerosmith, Fleetwood Mac, Led Zepplin, Judas Priest, Styx, Deep Purple, AC/DC, the Rolling Stones, the Beatles, and of course, Kiss.

I wanna rock and roll all night and party every day.
~ Kiss
Our story continues ~ trace.

Chapter Seven

LSD & Other Mind-Numbing Fun

The car seems to be going a wicked 102,
but the speedometer says a slow 32.
The air outside seems so one-dimensional.
A kaleidoscopic play of colors runs in a slow stream across
the night sky.
Cut-out trees of paper fly by as our priest-driving chariot
heads to where,
moves down the Green Street of this acid-driven ride maybe
to know where.
Reality speaks. "Trace, ya with us?" says the man counting
his fingers.
Of course, I am here. Where else could I be? Oops, where is
here?
~ trace, 1977

Seventy-nine years ago, an unsuspecting Albert Hoffman discovered a chemical substance that would alter the face of rock music and drug culture forever. While experimenting with the medicinal properties of lysergic acid compounds in the late

1930s and early forties, Hoffman ingested what would soon become known as LSD, a drug that came to define the latter part of the 1960s music scene.

The counterculture of the 1960s spilled over into the following decade, leaving a lasting impact on the drug scene and pop culture of the 1970s. I truly believe that the kids of Weymouth picked up the drug ball and ran with it well into the seventies, as we had a passion for drugs of all kinds.

The popularity of LSD expanded quickly in our gang and others of Weymouth during the summer between seventh and eighth grades in the early seventies. We all had a universal agreement to, as Joe liked to say, *take a trip and never leave the farm*, a quote made famous by the song "Wildwood Weed" by Jim Stafford. Yes, that summer, behind the old YMCA, we-soon-to-be eighth-graders took our first trip on LSD, or, as the Beatles called it, *Lucy in the Sky with Diamonds*.

We got a strong nod of approval from the entertainment industry, which fostered the youth drug culture through the imagery of rock music legends caught in the throes of drug addiction. Across America, drugs had become cool. Acid, weed, hash, Quaaludes, bennies, and black beauties were the drugs of choice in the small town of Weymouth.

While working late on *The Neighborhood Gang*, my thoughts turned back to a special trip, just one of many. Steppenwolf's "The Pusher" haunts the darkness around me: *But I've never touched nothin' that my spirit could kill.* I needed to call Joe about a special trip to make sure it even happened.

"Oh, yeah, Trace! That trip really happened!" was his response after I took us back to a moment in time of mind-numbing fun.

We're Back

The task took a bit longer than I thought. It should have been a quick run to a local restaurant on Bridge Street to meet Tommy in the parking lot and pick up our night of fun, but Tommy showed up an hour late. Thankfully, he did show.

"Man, where ya been? I been waiting for over an hour." I was a bit ticked off because I knew somehow this was going to be all my fault when I got back to the neighborhood, where Joe and Scott were waiting for me and the night of fun I had come to get.

"Sorry. My mother was watching me like a hawk tonight. Tough to get out here," Tommy spat back, all the while scanning the parking lot. Heck, maybe he was looking for his mother, or more like the cops, given what we were about to do.

"I gotta get moving," I said. "Me, Joe, and Scott got a trip to take. Do you have the stuff?" I reached into my pocket, pulled out fifteen bucks, and showed the money to Tommy, just in case.

"Got it right here." After looking around once again, Tommy opened his hand to reveal a small baggie holding three small square pieces of white paper. He snatched the money from me, shoved the baggie into my hands, and then strode away, heading around the building and out of sight.

Taking Tommy's cue, I turned and ran down Rosalind Street, back to the neighborhood with my precious cargo of the night's festivities.

"Trace, where ya been?" Joe yelled as I headed through the woods near Kathrine Street. "You left a week ago."

"Tommy showed up late. I got here as quick as I could." I stopped for a moment to catch my breath after the three-mile run I had just done at a pretty good clip.

"Did ya get it?" Joe asked as he and Scott, holding a joint, came out of the woods.

"Yeah," I said, thrusting out the baggie in my left hand. "Right here. Three for fifteen like we agreed."

Joe took the baggie from me, opened it, and took out the three squares of paper. He handed one to Scott and one to me, keeping the third for himself.

"So, wanna get electric and take a trip?" he said, smiling at the thought of the night before us. Placing the paper on his tongue, he grinned like the devil himself had just delivered the notice that a trip was at hand.

Following Joe's lead, Scott and I placed our squares of paper on our tongues and let the acid dissolve into our mouths. LSD, blotter, acid. No matter how you spell it, we were heading out for the night on the fifth trip of our lives.

Now, as most of us from back in the day know, the last thing you want to do is trip around non-tripping folks, so the three of us set out in search of a solitary place. We walked up Green Street and, when we came to the railroad tracks, took a left, heading toward the Weymouth dump and North High School.

The Old Colony Railroad started service in 1845 and closed in 1959. The railroad built small wood-frame depots along the track, which served as the station facilities. Anyone who has walked the tracks will tell you there is never anyone around on these tracks, making it a great place to get high or engage in any other less-than-lawful activities that kids tend to do.

After walking along the tracks down East Street, we came to the intersection of East and Wharf Street. Back in the day, about three hundred yards down the track stood one of the old depots. This is where we chose to complete our trip and never leave the farm. Taking our places on a bench at the far end of the platform, we let the drug take hold of our minds.

"Trace, are ya there yet?" Joe asked, nudging my arm. I was not sure what he meant by that; I was too busy looking at the one-dimensional tree slowly shaking across the tracks and the colors running across the sky in crazy patterns.

"Not sure, Joe, but I think I may be starting to see a few things. How about you?" When I turned toward Joe, I could see he was trying to either count his fingers or see how they moved, as he was turning his hand over and over while wiggling the fingers of his left hand vigorously. Scott, over at the far end of the bench, was blowing cigarette smoke into the air and laughing at the weird shapes his mind saw in the smoke.

We were off and running. The big bugs were crawling up our spines, and the big shivers were racing through us. And by "shiver," I mean we were really shivering, like we were cold, and then our shoulders would flex, our necks, too, as the spasms started to build. It feels like your mind is stumbling outta control—a little stumble at first, then another, and pretty soon, it's like you are falling down a flight of stairs. And just when you think you've finally come to the end, it kicks in again, even harder than before. Colors seem a little brighter, and you can hear little things in songs you didn't hear before. *"I buried Paul." Does anyone know what that's about?*

If you take too much, you can go full psychosis and see things melt. Sit under a tree and look up; it may smile back. You can even see music waves in the air. Honestly, you can see pretty much anything at this point. I didn't like seeing those giant turkeys with chainsaws.

As Joe would say, "We was trippin balls."

Just when I thought it couldn't get any weirder, it did. It was as if the rabbit hole opened and Alice came tumbling down.

A voice broke the silence of the night. "It's them! It's them!"

The three of us turned and looked down at the track. A small girl slowly came into focus, breaking the night that surrounded her. Around sixteen, with long brown hair, wearing a white shirt, blue jeans, and a blue windbreaker, she was running down the railroad tracks. She stumbled over the wooden rail ties and fell. After getting up, she fell again. I wasn't sure why she just didn't run on the side of the tracks, but hey, I was tripping. She continued to scream, "It's them! It's them!" as she ran blindly down the tracks toward us.

Scott and I just took this like it was part of the happening. Joe, on the other hand, ran out onto the track and stopped the running damsel in distress. Guessing the girl was tripping like us, he tried to console her. After a moment, Scott and I finally got up off the bench and walked over to see if it was really Alice. To this day, I think it was, which made me the Mad Hatter. Joe, no doubt, was the hookah-smoking Caterpillar, and Scott was the Dormouse.

"It's okay. You are with friends," Joe said as he tried to calm the girl.

"No, it's them! It's them!" the woman cried out. Breaking away from Joe's grasp, she sprinted down the track, tripping and falling as she ran.

We just stood there in the middle of the tracks for a moment, watching the girl disappear into the night. "Hmm, that was a bit weird," Scott said as we walked back to the bench. He lit a joint, sat down, and resumed watching the smoke make weird shapes. Joe and I followed suit and sat back down on the bench. Scott passed the joint to Joe, and nothing more was said about Alice and what we had just seen.

But that was not the end of the rabbit-hole theory as, about fifteen minutes later, it opened again. A *clunk-clunk, clunk-clunk* floated our way from the darkness down the track. After a moment, what appeared to be headlights appeared and grew closer as the sound became louder. Soon, it was right in front of us.

"Hey, you guys seen a girl running down the tracks?"

Past the lights, I could see someone calling out to us from a Volkswagen Beetle driving down the middle of the track.

"Yeah, she ran that way about ten minutes ago," Joe replied, pointing to where Alice had run. The car moved forward, and the *clunk-clunk, clunk-clunk* sound started again. After a moment, its taillights disappeared into the darkness, moving away into the whimsical world of Wonderland.

Scott passed me the joint. He didn't say a thing about what had just happened. "Trace, watch the shapes of the smoke. They are wild." Blowing the smoke from my lungs into the air, I watched in amazement as it danced into the night.

Later that night, we walked out of the rabbit hole and caught a ride to a local Chinse restaurant in Weymouth, as we now wanted to eat. Joe walked around the restaurant, shaking hands and announcing, "Good to see you. We're back."

Yes, we took a trip and never left the farm.

Jean

"Hey, Trace, can you get some acid?" Jean asked and then slowly kissed me. We were down at Julia Road Park, sitting on the bench. We had to leave in a few minutes to get her back home. Her mother had given us till ten o'clock, and I didn't want to be late, as this was the first time Jean had been allowed to stay out that late.

My mind was on first base, and maybe a bit more, but this girl was persistent. "Trace, can you get some acid?" Jean touched my thigh and flashed that wicked little grin of hers. Was this a promise of things to come?

I nodded and kissed her again. "Why do you want acid, anyways?" I asked, pushing my hand up her shirt just a bit. Her firm, tan belly felt amazing.

"I thought you and I could take some acid. I want to see what it's like." Touching my cheek, she kissed me again. A moment later, she pulled away. "We need to get going." She jumped up from the bench and slowly walked toward Julia Road, the start of the thirty-minute walk back to her house.

The deal was set. Next Friday, Jean would get some extra time out, and we would take a trip together.

"We're still doing it tonight, right?"

It was wicked-early Friday morning, and Jean had called. She had gotten permission for a midnight curfew that night. According to Jean, we were going to a friend's house for a party that would be supervised. At least, that is what she had told her parents, and they'd bought it.

A whisper came over the phone. "You got it, right?"

I hesitated before answering. Was I sure I wanted to take an acid trip with my girlfriend? Up till then, I had been on two trips with my friends as support. For this tri,p I would need to be the solo guide. Was I up to the task of taking Jean and myself through our minds?

One-dimensional trees of white shaking so fast they barely seemed to move. Clouds looking like they were sitting on glass plates as they passed through the colors running through the sky. The world looking like a cartoon, with strange and interesting textures, colors, and patterns. People turning into lizards or giant turkeys with chainsaws. Colors dripping down the walls. So many flames.

"Yes, Jean, I got it."

Jean and I had a date with Lucy.

Our trip started that Friday around four o'clock. We met up in Bicknell Square and quickly headed down past the drive-in and into the Rez. As we paused for a moment at the entrance down by Hingham Bridge, I gave Jean her first hit of acid.

"Time to get electric. Are you sure, Jean?" But it was too late as she took the small white piece of paper and quickly put it under her tongue. "Okay, I guess you don't need instructions on use," I said, placing the small white piece of paper in my mouth.

We had just taken microdots, more commonly called LSD, a wickedly powerful hallucinogenic drug that alters your perception of the outside world. LSD can turn you into a gibbering, giggling wreck, make the world seem like a magical place, or just plain take you to colorful places only your mind can go.

The clock was ticking. In about thirty minutes, the trip would start, with no stops for the next twelve hours. I would be with Jean for only eight of those hours. What was I thinking? Oh, I was a teenager at the time. I wasn't thinking.

"Are you feeling it yet, Donnie?" (*I hate that name*) Jean asked as she moved away from me to explore something she'd seen in the woods of the Esker.

I was sure the drug was working on me, as the trees we already turning two-dimensional and frosted a dead white. "Pretty sure I am there, Jean. And you?" But I already knew the answer. My date had found her fingers and the amazement of watching them move.

For the next seven hours, we wandered the streets of Weymouth, never staying in one place for too long as being around large groups got a bit weird and it became challenging to handle the stares, *real or not*. We never went to the one safe place we should have gone: the neighborhood, where, I am sure, a few other trips were happening. I tended to keep my dating scene out of the neighborhood.

At midnight, I walked her to her backyard. We laughed as we said our goodbyes, and then Jean entered her house.

The following day, Jean told me her parents had been in bed and only called out to her to say goodnight. Then she'd gone to bed, where she'd stared at the ceiling most of the night.

My editor reminded me that we took many more trips over the seventies: "You have many more books you could write about growing up in Weymouth." True enough. I wish every person I knew back in the day had the time to sit and chat about every moment we shared.

As the band 38 Special says, *So, take me, take me back to paradise, ooh*, the very next day, Jean told me she wanted to go back to Paradise. We never made it there as our time together was nearing an end on that cool night in August on the beach.

A few years later, Jean went back to Paradise with her new boyfriend and ran into the side of a fast-moving semi on Bridge Street that she had failed to see.

I haven't been back to Paradise since my lost years in the mid-eighties. The last time there almost killed me. I didn't care about life and never felt so alone out there in Sin City, and I thought a mix of heroin and cocaine would be a fun trip. That is when my soul was nearly lost. I will never know how I ever made it back. I do think most of us who took the trips to Paradise back in the day were explorers who craved pushing ourselves to the edge of music, drugs, and life.

To all my friends and the trips, we took to Paradise, one on one or in small groups, I wish I had the pages to jot them all down. I traveled so Bridges and rough twisted, one-dimensional trees and skies laced with running colors, talked with French fries with Roy W. at the King on the Street of Bridges, and watched a granite man float through with Claude and Kenny (*I'm pretty sure that was real, as all three of us saw it*). Unfortunately, I must end this chapter with so many of our stories left untold.

The list of songs I could end this chapter with, from "The Pusher" to "White Rabbit," would stretch for miles. But it seems appropriate to end this chapter with a song from a very local band. Aerosmith said it all: *You can't help yourself from fallin'. Livin' on the edge.*

Our story continues. ~ trace

Chapter Eight

The Oldest Game

Falling in love, the oldest game,
A feeling that's always been the same.
From the dawn of time, it's been around,
A feeling that's never been bound.
It's a feeling that's hard to describe,
A feeling that's hard to prescribe.
It's a feeling that's hard to ignore,
A feeling that's hard to deplore.
Falling in love is the oldest game.
~ trace

Back in the day, I always kept my love life away from my neighborhood life. I never brought a girl to the neighborhood, though any girl I dated knew of my life down across from Oats's house on Katherine St. During the summer months, most of my dating down on the New Beach was mainly with the gang. Some nights, I worked at my first real job, making pizzas up on Bridge St. It was hard work, but I always had some spending money. That made me a bit popular, mainly for beer runs and buying an ounce of pot, or as we would say back in the day, "four fingers for eighteen dollars." Yes, I said it right.

Back in the early seventies, an ounce of pot cost just that, eighteen dollars.

Despite my charming personality and good looks, it seemed the ladies of the gang never really paid much attention to me except for a nod or a simple acknowledgment of my presence. There was one exception: Tina. Our friendship grew stronger every day, and we were always together.

I always had doubts about my dating life because I didn't think I had anything to offer. My home life was terrible, my grades were poor, and I didn't have any special talents. I wasn't attractive enough to catch the attention of the girls in my group. But it didn't bother me because I never wanted to experience the heartbreak that always followed. Except for Tina, who was just a friend, I never saw any of the girls in my neighborhood as potential dating partners and never made an effort to pursue them.

Thinking back now, Joe, Oats, and Jim never dated the girls in our gang, either. Joe, being a rock star, always seemed to find a girl somewhere, but he never brought them to the neighborhood. Jim tended to keep his dates to himself, and Mark seemed to always be working, so I am not sure what went on with him and dating during our times down in the hood.

The year was 1972, and I found myself deeply infatuated with a young woman named Jean. The song "Smoke on the Water" by Deep Purple was all the rage during that enchanting spring. As the season unfolded, I bade farewell to the familiar surroundings of Bicknell and embarked on a new chapter at Weymouth North High School, where I would have to establish my social standing once more. Despite the challenges ahead, my heart was filled with love, and I held on to the hope of experiencing a deeper connection before the summer's end.

I met Jean in Tuesday's study hall, sixth period, down in room 105, I think, by the far-right entrance of Bicknell on the first floor. She sat in front of me and would turn around to talk to me and a few others when the teacher wasn't looking. It took me the better half of the school year to get up the nerve to ask her out.

As soon as I overheard that one of the other guys she was conversing with during our study period was planning to ask her out, I knew it was time for me to pull off my renowned move. Hastily making my way down the hallway after our last class, I was aware that Jean was heading to her homeroom before leaving for the day. "Jean, can we have a minute to talk?" I pleaded, more out of desperation than a genuine question.

The moment I caught her attention, the beautiful girl turned and gazed at me, her pretty smile adorning her cute face. Her eyes radiated mischief, a sparkle that I soon discovered would accompany us throughout our time together.

"Sure, Trace, what's on your mind?" I could tell that she already knew what I wanted to discuss, yet her smile persisted, radiating warmth and understanding. It was as if she had a sixth sense, effortlessly picking up on the thoughts and emotions that lingered within me.

As a shy schoolboy, I struggled to find the right words, stumbling over my tongue. The bustling hall echoed with the sounds of teens rushing to their homerooms, slamming lockers shut as they went. Jean, however, seemed to see right through me, her gaze fixed on the bustling crowd. Finally, I mustered up the courage to invite her to the baseball game that evening after school.

The situation seemed bleak until her gaze met mine, and she uttered those magical words: "I would be delighted to join you in watching the game tonight." And thus began a beautiful journey of love and growth that spanned a little over a year.

Isn't it time you took time to wait?
Falling in love could be your mistake
~ The Babys, "Isn't it Time"

It took me a solid two hours to gather the bravery needed for that first kiss behind Bicknell. While we walked down the green pathway, we engaged in endless conversation, feeling as if time stood still. The distant sounds of the ball game kept us company. I can't help but wonder how many breath mints I consumed during that magical late afternoon.

I shared the news about my lucky find of a girlfriend with Joe, Jim, and Oats that spring and asked for their opinions on the matter. Later on, I would rely on their approval of how awesome Jean was. She was incredibly attractive, and both Joe and Jim agreed, saying, "Yeah, she is nice, Trace."

Throughout the next year, our relationship blossomed. Every week, we would venture to Papa Gino's on Bridge St. and relish in the delight of two sodas and a cheese pizza for just a dollar.

As we sat at the table adorned with a vibrant red and white checkered tablecloth, we would carefully choose three songs from the jukebox, costing only a quarter.

Over time, I became a grill cook at the same spot, earning a modest wage of $1.65 per hour. This job was significant to me because it was my first step into the workforce. The two years I spent there were full of cherished memories that I will always treasure.

As I look back more on those two years, I realize how much I grew as a person and how the experience shaped me into the hardworking individual I am today. The lessons I learned and the memories I made will always hold a special place in my heart, and I am grateful for the opportunity to have started my career at that grill—and to Mike B. for all the time he took to help me get there.

Jean and I practically lived at Wessagusset Beach, spending most of our time chilling, swimming, and getting tanned.

When I wasn't at the beach or working, I would head to the neighborhood to hang out with the gang and get high every night. Around this time, I was pretty much homeless. I never told any of the gang, but Joe and Jim must have known, as they often offered to let me sleep at their houses.

I was in the ninth grade at the time, and at one point, I got a room up at Quincy Point for twenty-five dollars per week. Joe and I had convinced the lady I was eighteen so I could rent the room. Life was good for a few months until the lady found out my real age and I was asked to leave.

My relationship with Jean lasted two summers, but it ended abruptly when she decided to break up with me on the jetty connecting the two beaches. Her words, "I don't want to see you anymore," marked the end of my first love affair.

But as the years went by, I came to realize that sometimes, love stories are meant to be cherished for what they were rather than what they could have been. Jean and I had shared a beautiful chapter in our lives, one that had shaped us into the people we had become. And perhaps that was enough.

Throughout the years, Jean and I would occasionally run into each other, but our encounters never amounted to anything. Too much time had elapsed, and our dreams of rekindling the past remained just that—dreams of the past.

Edwin McCain's "I'll Be" plays softly as I write tonight:
"Tell me that we belong together."

Many of my dear friends from my past have managed to maintain a strong and unwavering bond with their first loves, even after more than forty years have elapsed. The love that flourished during the seventies was remarkably authentic, extraordinarily passionate, and eternally enduring. Embracing your first love meant immersing yourself in an ineffable sense of true love and bliss beyond measure.

Personally, I believe that love was more profound during the seventies. We used to spend a lot more time together as friends because that was the only option we had—simply hanging out with each other. Couples back then learned and evolved alongside one another. Making plans required careful consideration, as there were no cell phones to facilitate last-minute changes.

I'm young, I know, but even so
I know a thing or two
I learned from you
~ Nazareth, "Love Hurts"

"Trace, where ya been?" Jim called out as I walked into the neighborhood. Joe was busy bogarting a joint. After a moment, he passed it to Jim. I could tell by the way Joe was looking at me that he had something on his mind that we needed to chat about. But knowing Joe, he would get around to it in his own good time.

Sitting down on the log, I impatiently waited for Jim to finish his hit on the joint and pass it to me. Catch-up time was here.

There were times when I was allowed back into the family
home over on Frank Rd. over the years, but too much had gone
by for that ever to be my home again. Even when my parents
died, they made sure to tell me that Frank Rd. was never my
home.

I told Jim that I had spent the whole day at the beach with Mary. He then gave me a joint as we prepared for a long-awaited ride through the fog. Since I had been absent, it was my responsibility to catch up with everyone. From the looks of the group, it seemed like I had missed out on a lot.

The Wessagusset Beach docks were where destiny had brought Mary and me together as school had let out that year.

A few good friends of mine and I were down at the docks on Wessagusset beach, swimming with about thirty other kids, playing water tag, and just being young teens and enjoying life.

Like most summer evenings in coastal Massachusetts, the wind was sleeping, the ocean was a green-blue sheet of wet glass, and the heat of the day still lingered into the early evening hours as the sun settled in behind Great Hill overlooking the beach. The lifeguards had long since left the beach, so the "no running" rules had been tossed out the door.

The water was near high tide, and only an occasional ripple broke the glassy surface as small boats passed the beach, heading back to their berths at the local yacht club.

While swimming near the docks, trying to evade being tagged in the game happening around us, Mary and I accidentally collided with each other.

I'm gonna take a freight train
Down at the station, Lord
I don't care where it goes
~The Marshall Tucker Band, "Can't You See"

At that moment, a connection sparked between us, and a deep bond began to form. Mary's striking features, tall stature, tight curly hair, and smile were absolutely enchanting, and she captivated me from the very first hello. "Hi, I'm Mary. You're Trace, right?"

"Yes, that is my nickname, but it works." The game of tag was over for us as we climbed onto the dock and started to talk. The conversation would last for the next hour or so.

As the sun left the horizon and evening covered the sky with stars, I walked Mary back to the Birches. It was about an hour away, but as we talked, the walk seemed only minutes.

We paused at the end of her street and shared a tender goodnight kiss that left a lasting impression on me. As she turned to make her way home, our hands reluctantly parted ways. It was at that moment that our love story truly began.

Our love story blossomed, and over the next year, we made countless unforgettable memories that will always hold a special place in my heart. I realize now that I wasn't prepared for someone as extraordinary as her to come into my life, and I regret not being ready.

However, since I was mostly living on my own and my mom favored her boyfriend over me, I often found myself spending nights on Mary's parents' couch as well as Joe's and Jim's. Despite the unconventional living arrangements, our friendship and love for each other remained unwavering for the next year.

After talking Sox for a while, Joe brought up my lateness that night and then broached the subject that I knew was coming. "Trace, Mary has that girlfriend Shelly, right?" It was more of a statement than a question. I just nodded through the smoke as Oat had passed the joint over to me.

I could sense the direction this was heading. It had been a topic of discussion before but never fully explored. It seemed like now was the time to stop avoiding the questions regarding this matter.

As I passed Joe the joint, he asked me if she would like to go out with him. It was a simple question to respond to, especially since Shelly had been constantly urging me to introduce her to Joe for the past couple of weeks.

However, the dilemma was that for this to occur, I would have to bring Mary and Shelly into the same neighborhood to meet my friends. I dreaded the idea of these two worlds colliding, as the lies I'd told to one would inevitably clash with the truth known by the other.

"Na, I am pretty sure she wouldn't," I replied. The thick gray smoke floated slowly from my mouth as I tilted my head back.

"Oh, absolutely, Trace!" Joe exclaimed, flashing a wide grin as he kicked off an imaginary rock concert with his air guitar skills. Bursting into laughter, he proudly declared, "Trace, my friend, I am a true rock star!"

The rest of us couldn't help but join in the laughter and playful banter, teasing Joe as he carried on rocking with his air guitar.

"I will ask Shelly tomorrow if I see her," I said, trying wicked hard to stop laughing as Joe sang while passing the joint back to me.

"All right, Trace, the boys are back in town. If that chick don't want to know, forget her."

Almost everyone recognizes these words from "The Boys Are Back in Town" by Thin Lizzy, a rock band hailing from Dublin, Ireland, in the late 1960s. The song would forever solidify Joe and me as the epitome of "the boys back in town."

"More cowbell, please." ~ Christopher Walken, SNL

Shelly quickly agreed to the rock star's request. The date was set for Friday night, and the four of us had a case of beer and several joints. I had gotten Joe to move the date over to the sand pits and Julia Rd. Park, keeping my two lives apart.

We met Mary and Shelly at Julia Rd. Park later that week around seven, and boy, were they already heavily under the influence! They were both in a mischievous mood as well.

Joe showcased his wit and charm, impressing everyone around him. The beer vanished swiftly, leaving us in a joyful state. As the night progressed, Mary and I went our own way while Joe and Shelly ventured off for some lighthearted fun as young adults.

With a cheerful tone, Joe exclaimed, "Talk to ya later!" and then whisked the girl away into the night, both intoxicated and eager to discover the secrets of life.

As Mary held my hand, a smile played on her lips. She mentioned how Joe had no clue about what awaited him. I took out a joint from my pocket, lit it, and took a deep, satisfying drag. The night had started, and I couldn't help but smile. I passed the joint to Mary and watched her inhale deeply.

I used to always reflect on my life when I got high. These days, however, music has taken over that role for me. As I reminisce about this special night, the gentle melody of Better Than Ezra's "Good" stirs up nostalgic memories within me.

Back in the day, this song would have perfectly captured that nostalgic feeling for me. It reminds me of a time when my life was filled with uncertainty and I never knew if I would make it through each day.

Looking back, only five people truly understood me and what I was going through: Joe, Jim, Mark, Tina, and Mary. They were there for me during the toughest moments, helping me overcome my pain. Perhaps that's why I felt like I was leading multiple lives simultaneously. I never wanted my suffering to be evident to those around me. I'm grateful to all of them.

> *And be aware that there's not many there*
> *Who want to take time to sing and play*
> *An honest song for the people no more*
> ~ The Guess Who, "Glamour Boy"

Around eleven, we all met back at where we started. Joe and Shelly were sitting on the park bench, making out. "Hey, kids, having fun?" I called out as Mary and I sat down on the bench together.

"Ohh, yeah, we are having fun," Shelly called back, kissing Joe again and laughing even more. She rubbed his thigh. "Yes, it was a great learning experience."

"Shelly, we need to get home," Mary said. "My mom is going to kill us if we are any later." She kissed me once again and then took Shelly by the hand for the fifteen-minute walk to her house.

"Bye, Joe. See you soon," Shelly called out as she and Mary slowly headed back to the Birches.

Lighting a joint, I sat down next to the big guy, and we started passing it back and forth. After a few minutes, Joe asked with his typical JW smooth voice, "Trace, did ya get any?" He nudged me in the ribs. "Come on, Trace. Did ya?"

Mary and I had shared an intimate moment on a night filled with firsts and of the utmost significance to our relationship, but I never divulged any of that to Joe.

That night will always remain a treasured memory, an instance when love and affection blossomed like never before. Mary and I spoke of our love for each other that night as we embraced.

The moment I first saw Mary on the docks of our past, her infectious smile, the way her laughter danced through the air, and the graceful way she moved were all truly extraordinary. Through the highs and lows, the laughter and tears of my crazy life back in the days, she was my unwavering source of strength, my guiding light in the darkness of uncertainty. Mary, I am grateful for every moment we shared, every memory we created.

Unfortunately, our relationship came to an end a few weeks later, and we didn't have a chance to have a meaningful conversation again until that night in 1978 in my parents' backyard, although it was only for a short while. When I think back to that night, I can't help but feel remorseful for how immaturely I behaved toward her. As I reflect on my life, I acknowledge that this will forever be one of my biggest regrets.

Luke Combs's "Hurricane" plays quietly into the night as I write: "Hadn't had a good time since you know when. Got talked into goin' out with hopes you were stayin' in. I was feelin' like myself for the first time in a long time."

Shelly and I managed to cross paths again at a neighborhood bar in Quincy a couple of years later. Since my breakup with Mary, we hadn't really seen or spent much time together. After a fun-filled night of laughter and drinks, we found ourselves at my rented apartment in East Weymouth, where we spent the entire weekend together. We made a promise to meet again, but unfortunately, we never got around to fulfilling that promise.

After a few months, I was able to move into my very own apartment and little did I know that The Oldest Game would introduce me to the intricate world of adult dating and romance. "I gotta admit, I was completely unprepared for what awaited me." ~ trace

As I sit here, writing a few of these tales about The Oldest Game, I can't help but reflect on the past. It was in seventh grade at Bicknell when I first began to understand what love meant to me. I witnessed Eddie engraving "TLA Eddie & Donna" on the back of his wooden desk chair during a study period with Mr. Dolan as our teacher.

For those who have memories of Mr. Dolan, he never let anyone fail throughout his teaching career. He was renowned for being incredibly relaxed and was cherished by all those he had contact with. In short, he was *"just a great person."*

"Hey, Eddie, what does TLA mean?" I whispered, though I should have shouted, as this was not a quiet study hall today.

"Really? You don't know what it means?" "How can you not know what it means?"

"Nope, I really don't."

Pausing for a moment, Eddie looked at me, and I thought he was going to smack me. "It means "True Love Always,' you idiot!

During my time at Bicknell Junior High School, I witnessed numerous instances of young students openly expressing their affection for one another. It was truly heartwarming to see the genuine love that existed among the students there, and I can vividly recall at least thirty couples who were deeply in love.

Love and relationships were always topics of great interest and excitement within the walls of our school, creating a sense of unity and joy among the students during those memorable days.

"Hey, Joe, recall that hilarious moment when me, you, and Mark brought our dates to the Combat Zone to watch a porn movie at the adult theater when we were like eighteen or so? We didn't stick around for too long because the girls were ready to leave as soon as the old guy opened up his coat to them, ha-ha! Ah, those were the days, good times, indeed."

Remember the surest way to know that there was a new couple in town? The walk where the guy had his arm around his new girl and pulled her tightly into him as they paraded down the school corridors, her arm around his waist. Yes, this was the "hands off, this gal is mine" walk.

Nothing is more painful than first love. Teenage love is loving someone and not being able to stop no matter how many times they hurt you. It is saying forever and wanting it to be true but knowing it won't be.

According to the dictionary, teenage romance is the temporary love of an adolescent. I've come across a ton of information online that suggests that most of our relationships, which we thought would last forever, only last around six months. However, those were some amazing "TLA 4-ev."

Whispering secrets under the starry night sky behind Bicknell Jr. High, we defied the notion that nothing lasts forever. Our love danced to a melody only we could hear, a bond that grew stronger with each passing day. In this timeless embrace, they have yet to witness the magic we created together. ~ trace

But let me tell you, Weymouth was truly exceptional in every aspect. Love seemed to endure and flourish longer in this seaside town. Even now, I chat with friends who are still together with their partners from our time.

Love held immense significance during the seventies, a decade filled with enchanting melodies that beautifully conveyed our affection for one another and the enduring bond we shared.

Even after fifty years, these classic love songs have not lost their relevance or emotional impact. Songs like Elton John's "Your Song" or Paul McCartney's "Maybe I'm Amazed" transport us back to a time when love was pure, seemingly unbreakable, and brimming with hope for the future.

"My gift is my song, and this one's for you." ~ *One of rock's greatest lines.*

These timeless love songs continue to remind us of the everlasting love we have cherished throughout our lives.

Cause like a picture she was laying there
Moonlight dancing off her hair
She woke up and took me by the hand
~ Sammy Johns "Chevy Van"

Our story continues. ~ trace

Chapter Nine

My First Apartment

A Moment in 1975
After three days of drinking and drugging with Joe and
Skip,
I got this inkling to head on home to my apartment up on
Winter St.
So, I'm walking down Middle St., soaking in my own sweat.
More of a stagger,
head hung low. It's four or five in the mornin'; the thumb is
not working.
One of the few days I am not working at the joint up on
Bridge St, flipping burgers.
The sun's coming up, and the birds are out singin'.
Wend my way up that stairway, the elevator not working.
Sixty-three steps later, I let myself into my pad.
My clothes hit the floor piece by piece; I am five once
more.
Stretch out nice on the bed of water, a wave of nausea
arrives.
McKinley Morganfield already on the turn table,
And I just push that remote button to sublimity!

Listening to the sweet sculptural rhythms of Muddy
Waters's "Hoochie Coochie Man,"
Joined by bassist Willie Dixon and Little Walter Jacobs on
harmonica,
Minglin' with the traffic noises outside as the world starts to
wake to a new day.
Flick woooo ahhhhh, smoke drifts slowly into the air as the
weed cuts the waves.
The "Sweet Emotion" of Aerosmith pulls me through the
waves and back into my high.
I hear the door opening to my pad. I don't care.
Is it "Minstrel in the Gallery" by Jethro Tull?
The sweet sound of my first older lover, the dame from
across the hall, fills the air.
"Feel Like Makin' Love" by Bad Company consumes the air
As the dame takes the joint, takes a breast-heaving hit,
long and strong,
Bending down, kisses me deeply, pushing her tongue and
smoke deep into me.
Taking her clothes off, the dame slips into bed,
Wrapping around my body, quickly falls asleep.
"A Soapbox Opera" by Supertramp has begun.
I am getting older now. Life is now at full press.
Pushing my eighteen years to nineteen, then who knows?
Sooner or later, time's gonna take its toll on us all.

~ trace

I don't really understand why people choose to have their
own apartment. In my case, it was quite straightforward: I had
nowhere else to go. My mother prioritized her live-in boyfriend over me, her second oldest child. I eventually learned
the reasons behind this, but Joe advised me not to mention it
in this book. Perhaps I can share it another time. Regardless,

there I was, in my very first apartment: number 215 on Winter St., Weymouth, Massachusetts.

Despite its small size, the one-bedroom unit represented a significant achievement for me as it marked the first time I had my own place with a secure lock on the door. At just two days past eighteen years old, I'd proudly signed my first lease and finally had a place to call home.

It brought immense relief to no longer be homeless after a year of constantly moving between different places, such as Joe's house, then Lungs, the 3-A motel on Bridge St., the Local Motel on Washington St., and even resorting to sleeping on the floor of a gas station.

However, the toll of working late nights at the gas station five days a week was starting to affect both my physical and financial well-being.

I would start my day by walking and hitchhiking to work at 4:00 A.M. It was a one-hour walk/run to reach the restaurant on Bridget St. I would work there until 2:00 P.M. and then spend the rest of the night pumping gas at a gas station on Route 53 (Washington St.) from 4:00 P.M. until 12:00 A.M. This routine continued every day of the week, with occasional days off.

Today was a day off, and I was sitting in the rental office, counting out $450 for my first and last month's rent. Now we were about to do like fifty here. Sign here and here, now here, and now initial here.

"Here ya go, Mr. Tracey," the rental agent said with a smile, handing me my keys. I was shaking so hard at finally obtaining my first home—Trace's place, as it was about to be called by Joe, Lung, Oats, and many more over the next year. As I walked outside, Oats was waiting to give me a ride back to the neighborhood to show off my keys.

"Oats," I said, "come on in. Let's see my place." Yes, I had never even seen the apartment. A quick tour of my place confirmed that the apartment had a bathroom, living room, kitchen, dining room, and bedroom, which, in a few days, would see me on my first and only waterbed. *Hey, it was the seventies.*

Later that day, Joe, Oats, and Lung helped me move in. All I had were the clothes on my back, a sleeping bag, and a pony keg of Falstaff beer. Yes, that was pretty much it...but it was mine, and it was in my own f-ing place.

I realize now, looking back at that day, how scared I was when, after a bit of time, my friends told me they had to go home as it was getting late. Even when I was homeless and living on my friends' couches, their parents were still there to help guide me through the fear of learning to care for myself. As the door shut and my friends left for the first time in my life, I was truly alone.

For the first week, I pretty much just worked and worked, as I was now a renter and had bills to pay and a life to move forward. But life was much more fun now, and I knew I needed to furnish it with a few things: furniture, for one, and transportation, for two, so I set out to do just that. In typical trace fashion, *"I just did it."*

Furnishing a one-bedroom apartment for a newly turned eighteen-year-old proved to be quite a challenge. Heck, how much stuff can you buy at K-Mart, located right across the street from my new place, on a limited budget? *I had no idea how to keep a budget*, but first things first. I did not need a bed or a shower curtain; heck, I needed music.

Seventy dollars later, I had my first piece of furniture for my pad: a turntable that played records, eight-tracks, and FM radio all in one, along with two giant speakers.

Sitting against a wall, Falstaff beer in one hand and a lit joint in the other, I embarked on my first true solo musical journey with Fleetwood Mac's iconic album *Rumors*.

Flick woooo ahhhhh, the smoke gracefully danced in the air, soothing my troubled thoughts as the weed took hold. With each exhale, the smoothness of the Falstaff beer mingled with the lingering smoke. When I pressed the play button, the needle glided across the vinyl, filling the room with the nostalgic sound of my very first record on my new cherished turntable.

The enchanting melody of "Rhiannon" filled the air as I settled into my very first apartment. In a whisper, my best friend Music asked me, *"Would you stay if she promised you heaven?"*

"Yes," was my reply. I hit the joint again, and as the harshness moved on to mellow, I experienced a magical night, getting high, *"wicked high,"* creating memories of dreams that I hoped would last a lifetime.

> *All your life you've never seen*
> *Woman taken by the wind*
> *Would you stay if she promised you heaven?*
> ~ Fleetwood Mac, "Rhiannon"

A few days later, sitting against the wall in my living room, I couldn't help but bask in a feeling of achievement. My cozy home was gradually transforming, now featuring a turntable, a shower curtain, beautiful window curtains, and my faithful sleeping bag.

To add to the progress, a few dishes now lined my kitchen cabinets, giving it a touch of homeliness. With a newly acquired glass in hand, I took another sip of beer, relishing the satisfaction of building my own little sanctuary.

Little did I know, but my life was about to take an unexpected turn as a knock echoed through my door. This single knock would leave an indelible mark, altering the course of my existence in countless ways that continue to resonate even now.

As soon as I swung open the door, I felt transported back to the vibrant atmosphere of Woodstock in the 1960s. It was a surreal experience.

Unexpectedly, a young couple in their mid-twenties who happened to be my neighbors in apartment 217 had caught wind of the music and had eagerly come over to extend a warm welcome.

Their enthusiasm mirrored the free-spirited nature of that iconic era, and I couldn't help but feel a sense of camaraderie with them.

Harry and Diana, who were no longer married but still maintained a close friendship, were the names they went by. Diana had a captivating sense of style reminiscent of the classic sixties era. She wore a large, floppy brown hat that perfectly complemented her thick brown hair, which flowed past her shoulders.

The collection of beads and necklaces around her neck added a bohemian flair to her outfit, giving it a unique touch. The tie-dye shirt she wore was covered in a captivating blend of white, orange, and swirling blue, and it appeared that she'd chosen not to wear a bra. Her faded bell-bottom jeans hugged her hips, highlighting her curves, and she finished off her ensemble with twine-colored sandals.

But it was her eyes that truly captivated me. The small dark-blue dots arranged in a pattern around the outer edges of her eyes added an enchanting depth to her baby-blue gaze. And her lips, always adorned with a warm and inviting smile, were soft and full, making her even more irresistible.

On the other hand, Harry had a tall and slender frame. He wore jeans that fit him well, and his distinctive feature was a dark, Fu Manchu-style mustache. To add a touch of vintage flair, he sported an old tweed jacket, reminiscent of the fashion popularized by Sonny Bono back in the day. Completing his look, he wore a scullery cap, adding a touch of casual charm to his overall appearance.

"Hey, there. Welcome to the building! I'm Harry," he greeted me warmly as he shook my hand. His friendly demeanor was immediately apparent.

"And I'm Diana," she chimed in, her smile matching Harry's welcoming attitude. It was clear that they were a friendly duo.

Harry's next inquiry, "Do you experience a state of euphoria, dude?" sounded more like a laid-back remark than a straight-forward query. It appeared as if he was just engaging in conversation without any intention to pass judgment or create any pressure.

"Absolutely," I said with a slight smile. "I find myself with the opportunity to do so on a daily basis."

I couldn't help but be captivated by Diana. She had an indescribable quality that made her stand out. As time went on, I discovered that she was the true embodiment of the spirit of the sixties. She embraced life and love and viewed the world through a lens of compassion and empathy.

I will forever cherish her serene understanding of life and am so grateful for the long moments we spent together over several months.

Diana, you always keep popping up in my mind with thoughts of the moments we've spent together. I often find myself getting lost in memories when I pause and let my mind wander. Unfortunately, those cherished moments have now become distant memories of the past. ~ trace

"Alright, dude, let's head back to our place." With just a couple of strides down the hallway, I found myself transported to an entirely different realm. Even though I had never set foot there before, it felt like the summer of love had enveloped the atmosphere.

The symbols carved into the wall told me that I had arrived at the famous intersection of Ashbury and Haight streets.

This spot, located in the lively Haight-Ashbury neighborhood of San Francisco, is where the influential peace and love movement began in 1967. It was an exciting experience to be there at the moment I entered their apartment.

In the following months, we found ourselves getting high almost every day. Harry, who had moved out after about a week, was hardly around anymore. Diane, on the other hand, would often come over and request to sleep beside me, as she disliked being alone at night. Naturally, I would always agree to her request.

However, it was disheartening that for the initial six months, our relationship only revolved around sleeping together and nothing more.

"Hey Trace," said Joe, "just wanted to confirm that we'll be crashing at your place tonight after the show, right?" It was amazing how my place had become such a hit among my friends. "It's such a relief to know that we don't have to worry about heading back home on weekends, especially when we're in the mood for baking or simply want to unwind. I mean, who would want to leave such a cozy and welcoming atmosphere?"

" Absolutely, Joe!" I'd set up the chessboard on my recently acquired, second-hand booth table. My place now boasted a waterbed, a table with chairs, cups, and a few plates, and, of course, an abundance of music, beer, and marijuana. Regardless of how elevated we were, we always made time for a game of chess and a few joints.

Life was picking up its pace as we embraced our teenage years, constantly pushing boundaries. Our taste in music was expanding to include new genres, and our experimentation with drugs had now shifted towards LSD. *However, the details of that particular phase are better suited for a later chapter in this book.*

Collapsed laughter running, falling, drifting across the mine-
field of your thoughts dissolved, wondering: Who am I? Why
should I be alone, alone?
~ Ultimate Spinach, "Your Head Is Reeling"

At this point, my work hours at the burger joint had shifted from mornings to nights, causing a change in my schedule. To accommodate this, I decided to switch my shifts at the local gas station to whenever I wasn't working at the burger joint.

This adjustment greatly improved my life by allowing me more time for social activities, which had been a challenge due to my limited budget.

Unlike most of my friends, who were still in school and only had part-time jobs, I had the opportunity to earn some extra money.

The exception was Mark, who had a full-time job and a nice yellow Camaro to drive us around in—mostly to the dog track in Raynham, where he would blow most of his money. I never was much of a betting man, tending to save my money for the piss-warm beer served there. Trips into the combat zone in Boston happened a few times a month but were over quickly, as the women there liked expensive drinks and quickly made our money go away.

On a fun note, the apartment complex had a community pool for the residents and their guests. Well, one day, I had guests over—about twenty-five people just showed up to swim. I am pretty sure I didn't ask them over, but somehow, I did. The manager was very cool about it but made it very clear that two was the max I could have over at any one time after that.

But the pool became a great place to meet other residents of the complex, and for some reason, it seemed to be frequented by many single older women. This was where I met Linda.

Wearing a stunning black one-piece bathing suit, she asked me to take her to dinner on my motorcycle that night.

Following that encounter, a passionate affair unfolded between the two of us, lasting half a year. She was a breathtakingly beautiful older woman who captivated my heart and soul. Linda was patient with me to a fault in so many ways.

I'm pretty sure there were no less than six keys to my apartment, as it always seemed there were two people at my place when I wasn't. Thankfully, my bedroom did seem to stay off limits, but never the fridge, as beer was always missing and food never lasted.

It's funny how, when you start paying for things, they quickly become important. This was when I learned that money truly does not grow on trees. It never once occurred to me to save money as quickly as I got it; spending it seemed to be my only thought—on beer, music, and drugs, in no particular order.

The drinking age was eighteen back in the day. *What were they thinking?* My life just seemed to go with the moment. Even to this day, I tend to spend more than I save and never really think about getting old. *Hmmm, now what?*

I had now added a Honda 450cc motorcycle to my list of things. With it came many drunken rides home from many clubs and late-night parties. Somehow, I always made it back to my pad without a scratch despite the many blacked-out rides late at night.

I was now a man, but I was not ready for it. Paying bills never really made any sense to me, and I was always scrambling to get caught up, always slipping further behind. Like most of us, I got lost in drugs and booze. The difference was that I had no safety net to catch me like a parent or a home to go to if needed. There were many scary moments back then.

I found myself alone so much of the time like the last person to leave a party. The sad part was that I always left first and never quite fit in anywhere.

The dating scene was a bit expensive, and with no school time to break the ice with the girls, it was dinner and drinks or sitting at the bar for a few hours, checking out the ladies who were there.

I was always a bit too young, as most eighteen-year-old girls did not spend their time at the bars on Tuesday nights. So, most of the time, I just wound up drunk and driving home alone. But not all the time; there were times I didn't drive home alone, only to be too drunk for much else but falling asleep.

During my first apartment years, my friends never really spent the night or lingered for too long at my place unless it was the weekend. Instead, it was more of a quick call on my speaker, followed by a casual, "Hey, Trace, are you ready? We're here. Come on down."

Our lifestyle was always filled with activities and excitement, leaving little time for idle hanging out. Besides, most of the gang had school the next day, so staying over at my place was never a practical option.

It's quite amusing how some people may think that our lives resembled those of the characters in *That '70s Show*, where they lazily hung out in someone's basement, always getting high. That couldn't be more distant from reality. This book seeks to portray the true essence of our lives and the authentic emergence of seventies culture in a quaint Massachusetts town named Weymouth, not some made-up location with foolish youngsters following a scripted storyline.

Everyone is changing, there's no one left that's real
So make up your own ending and let me know just how you feel
~ Puddle of Mudd, "Blurry"

Our story continues. ~ trace

Chapter Ten

The Circuit

In that moment, the bars became a sanctuary, a haven
where time stood still and worries faded away. The combination of cigarette smoke, beer, and loud music created an
intoxicating blend that transported us to a different era,
where inhibitions were shed and memories were made. It was
a sensory overload, a sensory experience that etched itself
into our minds, forever reminding us of the vibrant nights
spent in that dimly lit, smoke-filled bar.
We were doing the circuit.
~ trace

The 1970s marked a pivotal period in Massachusetts and
the entire United States, one of remarkable transformations
in both the bar scene and music culture. This era witnessed
the rise of diverse bar styles, such as the iconic tiki bars and
sophisticated cocktail lounges from the 1950s, the rebellious
counterculture bars of the 1960s, and the vibrant disco bars
that defined the 1970s.

In the midst of this dynamic shift, Joe and I coined the term
"The Circuit" to describe a collection of clubs located on the
South Shore of Massachusetts, where Joe and his numerous

bands performed throughout the decade. Interestingly, the teenagers of Weymouth seemed to miss the disco fever and the grunge music craze, Instead remaining unwavering in their passion for good old-fashioned rock 'n' roll. This unwavering dedication to rock music further solidifies Weymouth's claim as the true birthplace of the seventies, as we proudly declare, *"Because we rocked and stayed."*

Replacing the jukebox. Bars and clubs in the 1970s discovered an important lesson in keeping their patrons engaged and drinking during breaks between live band sets or slow nights. Jukeboxes were not ideal as they played songs at a slower pace and sometimes people didn't feel like choosing songs. This resulted in less money being spent on drinks. To address this, disc jockeys, or DJs, emerged as a solution. In the 1970s, with the rise of rock 'n' roll culture, turntablism became a form of artistic expression.

One such DJ, known as ACE, or as I call him, Joe, started spinning the wax at various clubs and bars a few nights a week, keeping the crowd entertained, drinking, and dancing and encouraging them to stay longer at this rockin' watering hole. What this meant for me was more drinking time with friends.

Mark and I, and sometimes Hot Rod, made the trips to where ACE was spinning the wax three times a week. With Joe and the band playing another two nights and us getting high at least once a week in the neighborhood, being out six nights a week was not unusual for the three of us.

Casey's. In the groovy seventies, this spot was undeniably my ultimate destination on Saturday nights—as well as for many others on the South Shore—a haven from the realities of life where I could immerse myself in the enchanting melodies, herbal essence, and intoxicating spirits, leaving behind all my worries and getting lost in the rhythm of rock 'n' roll.

I've been talking with Joe the last few days, and our memo-ries are wild about this bar.

The reality was that the only bands I ever really heard there were ones Joe played in. But the beer was always wicked cold, the rum was tough, and the nights were always parties until the end.

Surprisingly, Casey's boasted only one restroom for each gender: two three-by-three rooms, both with non-working sinks.

Joe just reminded me that we used to call this place "Thee Dry Heave."

"Hey, Trace, listen to this!" Joe yelled out over the crowd as I walked through the door. He was already there, working. My friend and local rock star was a regular fixture at Casey's. When he wasn't rocking the stage with his band, he would take on the role of DJ, spinning vinyl records in between sets.

His passion for music was infectious, and he had an un-canny ability to read the crowd and play the perfect song to keep the energy alive.

Joe kept nodding for me to come up to the DJ booth. With a wave of my hand, I pointed at the bar, made a motion of drink-ing, and then flashed a peace sign for two to ask if he wanted one. Of course, he did. With that Joe smile, I knew it was a yes. I turned and headed to the bar.

I had walked in from another driving snowstorm and gotten to Casey's around 9:30. I did not have a car, so my thumb had gotten me there in ninety minutes or so after the bus ride from Quincey T-station to Hingham Center. *"Last stop. Every-one off."* Then I hitched a ride from the Hingham Rotary to Nantasket Beach Boulevard, where Casey's was located.

Joe was always the ride to somewhere later. Looking back on those days, what I wouldn't have done for a drink or some time away from reality into my own make-believe world, where I was doing fine and had the time. I never worried about later, just now.

Yes, time was doing what it always does: quickly ticking away. With only three hours left to drink, I needed to catch up, which meant I needed to make a dent in my wallet.

"Hey, Phyllis, two shots of Jack and two Buds, please," I called out to the bartender, whom I had grown to know after many a long night drinking at Casey's. Throwing a twenty on the bar with a "Keep the change," I grabbed the drinks and headed over to the DJ booth to start my drinking with Joe.

"Whaddaya think about the song?" Joe asked as I passed him a shot of Jack and a long-necked Bud. The song was "TV Is King" by the Tubes, the first time I had heard them. Thankfully, it would not be my last, as the Tubes quickly became one of my favorite bands of the seventies. *"You're just a tube full of gas and a box full of tin."*

The shot hit the spot, and the cold started to slip away. "Who was that?" I yelled above the next song, another favorite of mine, Kansas's "Point of Know Return." As the song belted out over the speakers, *"You cried with fear, the point was near,"* the crowd, closing in on their own point of no return, called out for more.

"The Tubes, 'TV Is King,'" Joe yelled above the noise. "The Point of Know Return" ended, and BTO quickly followed—we were now "Taking Care of Business."

"Trace, ya wanna stay at my place tonight?" Joe asked, knowing that was my idea as, at the time, I was close to homelessness and spent most of the time at my grandmother's place over in West Roxbury.

"Yeah, that sounds great. I won't have to rush to catch the last train outta Quincy."

The next song to hit the turntable was "Radar Love" by Golden Earring: *"Radio's playing some forgotten song. Brenda Lee is comin' on strong."* The crowd was getting amped up as the hits continued.

"I really need to get a place on the South Shore," I called out.

Jody kind of walked up to the DJ booth, more of a stagger, really. *Jody always had the greatest smile, and those bedroom eyes were to die for.*

"Hey, Trace, can I talk to ya for a minute?" she asked with a wave of her hand. I could tell she was wicked trashed just from her smile.

After climbing down from the booth, I moved up close to Jody so we could talk over the noise. The next song was playing, Van McCoy's "The Hustle." *Just kidding,* Cheap Trick's "Surrender" started, *Live from Budokan:* *"Mother told me, yes, she told me I'd meet girls like you."* This place was jumping like it was the best live performance by the boys themselves ever.

"Hey, Jody, long time no see. How ya been?" As I gave Jody a big hug and kiss, I could smell the pot and taste the beer. Yes, I was right. This friend of mine was trashed. But then again, who wasn't in this place tonight? That was why we came there in the first place.

"Good, Trace. I need a favor. I want you to help me hook up with Joe tonight," Jody told me with that wicked smile of hers. "Bang a Gong" by T-Rex was tearing into the smoke and flashing lights in the club; this place was a-rocking. *"Well, you're dirty and sweet, clad in black, don't look back.*

"You know Joe, Jody. Just go talk to him. He is pretty trashed. I am betting he will say yes." Turning back toward the booth, I saw Joe had lit a joint and was passing it down to me. I took it, inhaled a huge hit, and smiled at Jody. Then, moving my lips close to hers, I slowly blew the heavy smoke into my dear friend's open lips.

"Shotgun!" Jody screamed as the smoke made its way to her mouth, our lips touching slightly. After a moment, she released the smoke and continued her plea for a night with Joe. "You and Joe are best friends, and he is a rock star. I always wanted to kiss a rock star." She waved to Joe as he took the joint back from me.

"Let's move before they raise the parking rate." "All Right Now" by Free was next to keep the crown moving and grooving. Joe worked quickly to load "What I Like About You" by the Romantics onto one of the dueling turntables.

"I will let Joe know of your hot love for him, Jody." With a smile, I kissed my dear friend and climbed back into the DJ booth to let Joe know of his great luck as a rock star. *"Tell me all the things that I wanna hear 'cause that's true."*

"Hey, Joe. Jody wants a kiss from you, as you are a rock star." Taking the joint from Joe, I took another hit and felt the smoke wash over me. The warmth was starting to take hold, and the cold from outside was a thing of the past. I felt so tired and alone.

Thin Lizzy's "The Boys Are Back in Town" began to play. Yes, the boys were back in town, down at Casey's Bar and Grill. *"If that chick don't want to know, forget her..."*

Another night at Casey's. On this cold December night, the drive down to Casey's on Nantasket Beach took some time. A typical nor'easter was dumping blinding snow at a wicked clip on the roads, bringing most traffic to a stop.

However, Oats and I were determined to make Casey's that night, as music, women, shots of Bacardi, and long-necked buds were on our minds.

Oats's yellow Camaro was sliding all over the streets as we hit the Hingham rotary at a brisk twenty miles per hour. "Trace, hold this." After handing the lit joint over to me, Oats tried to get both of his hands on the wheel for the turn through the rotary.

I inhaled deeply from the joint. Holding my breath tightly, a mix of fear and anticipation filled me. Oats suddenly stepped on the gas with a determined "F...CK this," causing the bright yellow Camaro to smoothly slide through the rotary. Our adventure continued as we headed towards Casey's down on the beach.

Twenty minutes later, Oats and I pulled into the already-full parking lot just across from Casey's. The Atlantic Ocean had blown the lot clean of all the snow, leaving a sloppy coat of black ice.

After passing the joint a few more times, I could tell we were really high. It wasn't even that late, around 9:30, but who cares? It was time to have some fun. We got out of the car, hunched over, and hurriedly walked the remaining fifty feet into Casey's.

"Come Here" was playing as we paid our five dollars and entered, escaping the bone-numbing cold. We made our way to the bar, where I ordered a couple of Buds and, as Joe would say, *"two shots of Jack Attack."* I handed Oats his shot and beer, and we quickly down the shots to help ward off the cold (wink).

Turning towards the stage, I could barely make out Joe. He was decked out in tight blue pants and a satin shirt, belting out "Lonely Boy" by Andrew Gold.

"Hey, Mark, why does Joe shop for girls' clothes to wear on stage?" I yelled over the music to Oats. I needed the right answer because, at some point, Joe would always ask me what I thought of his outfit that night.

"Beats me," Oats yelled back before taking a long swig of his Bud. "Must think he is sexy in them, I guess." Then he walked away as someone in the crowd called out his name.

Turning back to the stage, I could see Joe's girlfriend, Toni, walking slowly through the crowd toward me. Man, she was so hot she could melt away the cold outside. *"I was a high school loser, never made it with a lady...*" The band filled the bar with the beat of "Walk This Way" by Aerosmith.

"Trace, glad you finally got here," Toni yelled out. The crowd began to scream as the band quickly started the next song, "Don't Fear the Reaper." "Joe was worried you weren't going to show tonight."

As I took a long swig from my Bud, I decided to offer up Oats as the reason we were late. "Oats drives like my mother in the snow," I called above the blare of "Don't Fear the Reaper." *"Come on, baby...don't fear the Reaper."*

"Joe wants to know if you two are still on for chess tonight after the gig," Toni said above the roar of the crowd. She lit a joint and inhaled deeply, her wicked-big breasts heaving in the air in her tight black shirt. Holding her breath, she passed the joint to me.

"I'm in for the game," I called out and then sucked deeply on the joint. The rush hit me like a freight train. I handed the joint back to Toni as she exhaled out the harsh smoke.

"Hey, Toni. Joe sounds great tonight," Oats said as he returned with three Buds in his hands. He handed one to Toni and one to me and kept the third for himself.

"Want some?" Toni asked, passing Oats the joint. He leaned back a bit and took a wicked-deep hit.

"Oats, can you give me a ride home tonight after the show?" Toni asked.

Sure, no problem," Oats replied. Passing the joint to me, he said, "Let me guess. Joe and Trace are playing chess again after the show."

I took another long drag from the joint. As I held the thick smoke in my lungs, I felt the enlightenment reaching into every part of my body. Blowing the smoke out slowly, I smiled a bit and said, "Not just chess, but drunken chess."

"Walkin' along the river road at night, barefoot girls dancin' in the moonlight." Creedence Clearwater Revival's "Green River"

filled the night. Looking up at the stage, I watched as Joe gave me the thumbs-up for our chess match.

Later that night, like the thousand nights before and the thousand nights after, Joe and I grabbed a few beers and sat in my mother's dining room, playing chess from 2:00 A.M. until the sun rose and beyond. In addition, every morning, my mother would make us breakfast and ask who won.

Joe, recall when we tried to prevent ourselves from falling by stapling our suspenders to the bar top? It was a valiant effort, but unfortunately, it didn't quite work out as planned. At least we can say we gave it our best shot!

A place on the pond. The drinking age was eighteen, and Joe and I were eighteen, and I had my own apartment right down the street and a Honda 450 cc motorcycle, so we were pretty much set to party when I wasn't working two jobs to pay my bills and earn partying money. We were regulars, and this place was always hopping with music and older ladies. The happy hours were filled with rum and Cokes for the asking. Add to this one great pepperoni pizza, and you had Joe and I for customers nightly that summer of '75.

We were at a lounge called The Water's Edge, over by Whitman's Pond. Joe, Hot Rod (Dick Smith—*miss you every day, Dick*), Oats, and I were totally trashed, even for us, on the edge of total blackness. For some reason, there was no air conditioning in the joint that night, and the place was packed to the walls with hot, sweaty women and us. Cigarette smoke filled the bar, and the noise was deafening.

As we, the mighty "Neighborhood Gang," guzzled down rum and Cokes and grooved to the tunes of a kickass local band, a sudden realization struck us like a lightning bolt. "Where the heck is Joe?" Hot Rod hollered from the other end of the table, leaving us puzzled.

Oh, boy, did I have insider information on the whereabouts of the big dude! There I was, chilling in my comfy chair, grinning from ear to ear. I had a front-row seat to Joe's epic journey of stumbling up those three measly steps leading to the dance floor and the band stage at the other end. It was pure entertainment, my friend!

Joe was now beyond smashed and wobbling and teetering around on the dance floor, completely alone. In one hand, he had a Bacardi shot, and in the other, a tall bottle of Bud.

The band had yet to start the second set after a quick break. Clad in his famed farmer-Joe overalls and flip-flops, with no shirt on, Joe screamed out, *"CUT THE CAKE...PLEASEEEEE!"* Turning back to the table, he gave me the famed J.W. smile that said, *"Don't worry, Trace. I got this."* Then he turned back to the band as they began to pick up their instruments and screamed out again, *"CUT THE CAKE...PLEASEEEEE!"*

The lead singer laughed and shook his head a bit. Then he shouted to the band, "One, two, three..." and the lead guitar started, followed by the four-piece brass sections a few seconds later. Joe started to dance by himself as the band began to wail "Cut the Cake" by AWB.

If you recognize that band and their song, then you were right there with us in spirit at the lounge by the pond that night, and we had many more unforgettable nights together.

The Ranch House. Back in the day, this place, down on the beach in Marshfield, was where you went for some of the best upcoming bands on the South Shore of Massachusetts. I stumbled upon this place during the Kashmir days of bands Joe was playing with. A very talented group of musicians had cut or were working on the album *First Dream*. I have to tell ya, this place rocked from the second you walked in to the moment you left to watch the fights in the parking lot. Rock *was the walk* of this place.

On weekends, it was pretty common to have two to three hundred folks show up. Sometimes, that also meant you had two to three hundred *guys and gals* duking it out in the parking lot, but hey, that's a whole different story. The ranch on the marsh made Patrick Swayze's bouncer movie *Roadhouse* seem tame in comparison.

The Ranch House focused on live music, much like The Rat (Rathskeller) music venue in Boston, a place that many consider to be the "granddaddy" of Boston rock venues. Maybe, but not everyone cared to drive to Boston when you could hear some of the greatest rock bands that had yet to make their mark playing to a screaming crowd down on The Ranch in a town the locals called "Marsh Vegas."

The entrance fee ranged from two to three dollars, depending on the band performing that night. You could be sure that once the music had started, everyone in the crowd would be up on their feet, dancing.

A place like The Ranch House would be wicked hard to find nowadays. No, it would be impossible to find.

Our memories are perfectly tailored to the beginnings of our youth, filled with moments of love, dreams, and so much more. They hold the essence of our past, capturing the essence of who we once were and the experiences that shaped us. ~ trace

Back to the place on the pond. At some point in the seventies, for some unknown reason, the drinking age was lowered to eighteen. Yes, what a great idea. So many of us started drinking legally around 1973. Thank God it was much easier to have older friends get your booze from the local packies.

Okay, so for all you non-Boston folks, I will give you a quick story about packies. *The term "package store" came out of the temperance movement even before the Prohibition and the Volstead Act of 1919. Drinking was often frowned upon in polite society, and a "proper Bostonian" saying was, "Never drink alcohol before 5 P.M. or East of Park Street," meaning the approaches to Scollay Square, a bit of a bawdy area popular with visiting sailors. Being in possession of alcohol, even in sealed containers, could get you stopped by police. In order to transport liquor discretely, stackable boxes were used, wrapped in brown paper and taped or tied shut with a string so you could get it to the privacy of your own home. Thus, "getting a package" became the euphemism. The Boston lingo made that "packie" over time. "Because we say so."*

The Water's Edge never seemed to slow down. Every night of the week, it was packed. How did I know that? Well, I think I was there every night. If I wasn't there with Joe, I was with my cousin Tommy or my older cousin Kevin, who both worked with me down at the gas station and lived near my apartment at the time.

My times with my cousins were important to me, as it seemed they were my only family members who cared if I lived or died back in the 1970s. In typical Boston fashion, all we did was bust on each other and other family members as we drank the night away at the place by the pond.

Basically, I was at a one-year party around this time, working all day and partying late into the early morning hours non-stop. I discovered my admiration for mature women at the pond, where many of the ladies fell within the thirty- to forty-year-old range. Divorce was common among them, as I listened to tales of heartbreak, children, work, and the people responsible for their pain. The funny thing about all these nights at the place on the pond was that never once did I leave with anyone unless I had brought them there.

I know it's too late now
But I wish I could go back in time
And start all over somehow
~ Jefferson Starship "Find Your Way Back"

Throughout the following year, I made it a point to visit as many clubs as possible to soak in the music, the company of girls, the excitement, and the thrill of smoking weed and tripping down the highway of acid, only to find myself facing the harsh reality of loneliness.

I wasn't prepared for any of it, but I managed to push through. Having friends like Joe, Jim, and Mark by my side was crucial, yet when night fell, and I climbed the stairs to my apartment, I was left to face things alone.

But I did find solace in the quiet moments of reflection that followed those wild nights out. I would sit on my balcony, staring out at the lights of Weymouth, contemplating the meaning of it all.

Was I truly happy in the midst of all the chaos and noise? Or was I simply trying to distract myself from the emptiness that lingered within?

It is late here. As I write, "Good Loving Gone Bad" by Bad Company plays quietly in the background. Man, I need to turn this up: "Now, I ain't complaining, just tryin' to understand."

Authentic rock 'n' roll blending soulful vocals and guitar riffs...it embodies the raw essence of the working class, exuding blue-collar grit and undeniable swagger. This music inspired me to start playing the guitar thirty-four years ago, I felt compelled to learn and immerse myself in its power... I simply couldn't resist the call of the music. ~ The Strick on Bad Company

Beachcomber ~ Nothing quite said "party to the edge" like this place. On the waterfront of Wollaston Beach in Quincy, this club brought hard-hitting, local rock 'n' roll bands that had a future in music. If ever I was going to lose my life because of drinking, this was the place it would happen. It's not that the club did anything wrong—because they didn't. It was just how the club affected me. Blackouts were common. Not remembering past eight o'clock at night, though we closed the club at 2:00 A.M. How many nights did I wake up, looking in my bathroom mirror and asking myself what had happened the night before?

The Beachcomber was a rare gem among nightclubs, with an unmatched ability to capture the essence of rock music. The hazy atmosphere, filled with smoke and the scent of beer and pot, combined with the absence of a proper air conditioner during the summer months, seemed to induce just the right amount of perspiration in the patrons.

Although the venue was always bustling with eager listeners, it was never quite spacious enough to accommodate the crowd. The roofs always felt inadequate, and the restrooms were too small to handle the influx of people.

Surprisingly, the Beachcomber also boasted one restroom for each gender. Its closing time was one o'clock, with a last call at 1:15 A.M.

I used to stick around with Joe and his rock band, who played gigs wherever they could make some cash. We traveled up north and ended up in some wild spots like the Beachcomber in Quincy and the Channel Night Club in Boston, along with other intense rock 'n' roll joints along the North Shore of Massachusetts. We never left any of these clubs without being completely trashed. Somehow, we always made it back to the safety of the neighborhood.

Years earlier, my cousin Kevin had a close brush with death when he crashed his Rally Sport Camaro into the sea wall near the Beachcomber after a night out with his friends. The accident left him hospitalized for nearly six months. Unfortunately, he never fully regained his ability to walk properly.

In the hushed darkness of the Tex-ass night, I find myself sitting in solitude, bathed in a dim glow that spills over my keyboard. The somber tune softly reverberates within the corridors of my thoughts, carrying me back to a bygone era. As I shut my eyes, the music swells, enveloping me in the otherworldly harmony of my youthful days. Originally performed by the renowned American country musician Jerry Jeff Walker, this heartfelt melody was immortalized in 1969 by the Nitty Gritty Dirt Band. It's none other than the poignant ballad "Mr. Bojangles," and even now, after all these years, I still mourn the loss of my faithful canine companion.

He spoke through tears of fifteen years how his dog and him
Traveled about The dog up and died, he up and died
After twenty years, he still grieves
~ Nitty Gritty Dirt Band "Mr. Bojangles"

Most of the gang members never really made the trek to clubs north of Weymouth, preferring to head south toward Hull, where Casey's, the Ranch House, and the Surf Club were located. How many nights did a short but great relationship with a beautiful lady begin there, with dancing, laughing, and falling in love so quickly—but then ending just as quickly?
When you take me by the hand

Tell me I'm your lovin' man
When you give me all your love
And do it, babe, the very best you can
~ K.C. and the Sunshine Band, "That's the Way I Like It"

The Surf Nantasket Ballroom quickly became a legendary venue for rock music in the 1960s and 1970s, hosting iconic bands such as The Doors, The Rolling Stones, Led Zeppelin, and, of course, Aerosmith. The energy and excitement of the performances at the Surf Nantasket Ballroom were unmatched, with the crowd often dancing and singing along to their favorite songs.

As the popularity of rock music continued to grow, the Surf became a must-stop destination for up-and-coming bands looking to make a name for themselves. Local acts, as well as national touring bands, all graced the stage at the Surf, creating unforgettable memories for both the performers and the audience.

Despite changing musical trends and the passage of time, the Surf remains a cherished part of Hull's musical history. Its legacy as a hub for rock music lives on, with many music fans still reminiscing about the unforgettable concerts and experiences they had at this iconic venue.

Labor Day 1976 marked the opening of Uncle Sam's after the Surf shut down, transforming into a disco before reverting back to its rock roots in the eighties. Uncle Sam's became one of the most popular nightclubs on the South Shore during the seventies and eighties, and I believe the club could hold well over a thousand rocking, rowdy, dancing, let's-spend-the-night-together patrons.

Joe and I—and sometimes with Mark—frequently made the trip to Uncle Sam's, mainly to check out the local competition to the band Joe was currently playing in. On a fun note, Joe had enough pull so we could walk in during the day and chat with some of the bands as they set up and practiced.

I frequented this club with a lady I was dating at the time. She was pretty, sincere, and loved to dance. We hit it off immediately, and things got intense just as quickly.

I can't quite recollect the exact details of our encounter, nor can I truly fathom the precise moment our connection diminished. It was an exhilarating experience, one that had the potential for blossoming affection, yet it came to an abrupt halt on that swing set close to the concession stand at the Braintree drive-in. *Even in your absence, life carries on for those intertwined with your existence.* Should this beautiful lady from yesteryears stumble upon these words, she'll comprehend the sentiment and sadness of this paragraph.

Uncle Sam's place had a crazy amount of stairs leading up to the main floor. It felt like there were twice as many stairs to go down after a night of partying and drinking.

Yeah, I'm gonna tell my tale come on, uh come on, give a listen
'Cause I was born lonely down by the riverside
~ Bob Seger *"Ramblin' Gamblin' Man"*

Our story continues ~ trace

Chapter Eleven

Don't Bogart That Joint

Roll another one
Just like the other one
You've been holding on to it
And I sure would like a hit
~ Little Feat

"If you don't get high the first time you smoke, you're prob-
ably doing it wrong."

Marijuana exploded on Weymouth in the 1970s. You could get an ounce of cannabis for about $18. Half of the bag was mostly brown, pretty seedy and stemmy, but the buzz was definitely there. As the drug was illegal everywhere, most of it came from other countries, like Colombia. Dealers knew the demand was greater than the supply, so they could provide less-than-perfect herb.

It's a fairly accurate assessment to say that the kids of Weymouth smoked it all, from the stems to the popping seeds, including the leaves of *any color* and, of course, the buds.

While the rolling of the joint and the kick from the smoke now are nowhere near what they used to be—or *so I am told, wink*—the weed now is much better than back in the day. Granted, cannabis started in the sixties, but it flourished into the seventies and beyond.

So began a wider, all-consuming recognition of a period marked by the distinctive character of radical change. A plant with over five hundred chemicals in it, some of which alter your mind and mood, became the subject of a national debate. Years later, this national debate would give legitimacy to the mainstream medicinal plant we have today.

It's funny how we folks of the seventies still prefer to buy our pot from a local dealer, even though, since 2016, you can walk down the street and buy weed from a cannabis dispensary. For some reason, you can legally buy weed, but publicly consuming it is prohibited. No, you can't smoke a bowl on the sidewalk. It's not like smoking a cigarette. It certainly is more fun, though.

One toke over the line Waitin' for the train that goes home, sweet Mary
Hopin' that the train is on time
~ Brewer And Shipley, "One Toke Over the Line"

Brands of the 70s. I never really knew what kind of weed I was smoking. It didn't matter who I got it from or who I shared it with as long as I got high. The best part of being high was the company of my friends and the laughter that flowed. We believed that getting high was all about having fun.

However, everyone wanted their pot to be the best, so different names were given to the brands of weed to signify their quality and potency. These are some of the names of the weed I smoked during that era: Maui Wowie, Acapulco Gold,

Colombian Gold, Panama Red, Afghani, Mazar I Sharif, Red or Blond Lebanese, Haze, Skunk #1, and Thai Stick.

Joe and I bumped into some real Thai Stick late in the seventies, somewhere deep in Boston, and I "gotta tell ya," when inhaling the rich smoke of those opium-dipped sticks, "I felt like I was getting high for the first time once again!"

Think I'll roll another number for the road
I feel able to get under any load
Though my feet aren't on the ground
~ Neil Young, "Roll Another Number"

Brands of today. I must admit that I haven't tried any of these brands myself, but not because of any particular reason aside from the names. However, based on conversations with younger individuals who are knowledgeable about smoking, it appears that these newer strains of marijuana can provide an experience similar to the potency of acid trips in the seventies. Interestingly, the research I conducted for this book suggests that today's marijuana is approximately 70% stronger than the varieties available during the seventies. In fact, the appearance of current marijuana plants is so different that they barely resemble the leafy friend we knew from that era. Some of the popular brands today include Gorilla Glue #4, Super Boof, Cap Junky, Bubba Kush, White Widow, Super Silver Haze, Trainwreck, G.O.A.T. Milk, Granddaddy Purple, Green Crack, Jealousy and Friends, Cheetah Piss, Cat Piss, Alaskan Thunder Fuck, Shark Breath, Milf, Herojuana, Zombie Death Fuck, Cougar Milk, and Purple Urkle, among others.

As Robert Plant was to say onstage in 1971, *"It was dedicated to 'the days when things were really nice and simple, and everything was far out all the time.'"*

How we rolled a doobie in the seventies. The word "doobie" is a slang term for a joint. I think we used the term to be cooler than the next kid. I always found *"Let's spark a jay"* to work just fine, as it always got the joint rolled and I was cooler than the other kids—*WINK*. I never was any good at rolling, so I either bought my pot as rolled joints from other kids for a few bucks each. If I did buy an ounce, I would ask one of the pro rollers in the gang to *"roll a fatty"* for me as I tossed them the bag with some E-Z Wider papers to use.

Sure, other forms of smoking devices, like pipes and bongs, came along later in the seventies. But papers were easy to hide, and you could always tell the cop who searched you they were for rolling cigarettes. Back in the seventies, a cop could just search you because he said so. Trying to spout off to the law back in the day was never a good idea. If the cop didn't, your dad would smack you for mouthing off to a cop.

Respect still lived for officers, teachers, parents, and anyone else your parents told you to have respect for. This was never up for debate; your dad was the man you listened to.

Oh, take your time, don't live too fast
Troubles will come, and they will pass
~ Lynyrd Skynyrd, "Simple Man"

My favorite rolling paper was E-Z Wider, mainly because they were plentiful and always in stock. The downside was that they tended to rip more easily than some of the other brands, but in a pinch, they worked fine.

Besides weed and rolling paper, the most important thing for building the perfect joint was saliva. Now, I know my friends from back in the day are smiling a bit because we all remember this most important part of doobie making. Of course, you needed pot, rolling papers, and a lighter, but you still needed to hold all this together, and the glue to make this happen was saliva, the *"spit"* of the person rolling the joint.

I can't tell you how many times I watched the roller soak the joint they were rolling with lots of their spit, stuffing the joint deep into their mouth. Some of the joints were soaking wet as they slowly pulled the joint out again. *Ugh, what were we thinking?* That is an easy question to answer: we weren't thinking. We just wanted to get high.

When I think about it now, I'm certain that I never constructed a joint in this particular manner, so nobody has really had a taste of my saliva.

The seventies saw influential figures, music, and social change shaping the weed culture, making it "COOL" and promoting acceptance of new experiences and perspectives. This shift in mindset allowed marijuana to establish itself as a significant presence that continues even today. ~ trace

Bongs and Pipes. Neither of these ever really made it to the neighborhood, mainly because both are indoor devices. Walking around with a bong would get you a few questions from the local authorities as to why you needed this device in the first place. There were always stories that bongs and pipes were illegal. Some people with the *"legal schtick"* would always show up in the neighborhood like a traveling legal representative to tell us things like, "Bongs and pipes are illegal. Even though you might see them on sale at Wooden Ships and other head shops, don't be fooled; these smoking devices are against the law."

I always found bongs and pipes more suited to smoking hash, and I am pretty sure I never smoked pot in one. I did, at times, smoke hash through a water pipe. That was fun, though I don't know if it helped the high or not.

Heck, in the service, we made potatoes and soda cans into hash pipes to smoke some of the best blonde hash I had ever smoked while in Europe. Nothing like being high on hash and playing a game of chess on a ship in a raging storm on the Atlantic Ocean with the battalion commander and kicking his butt. Anyone who has ever played me in chess—*ask Joe*—will tell you I only play for keeps.

The world
And the world turns around
The world and the world, yeah
The world drags me down
~ The Cult, "She Sells Sanctuary"

It's getting late in the evening here in the great state of Texas, and I'm just enjoying some coffee, my new favorite pick-me-up. I'm reminiscing about the times when I used to indulge in the "herb" and wondering how many people could get high from just one joint. I think maybe around five unless Joe was one of them; then it would probably be three at the most. You were always the best at finishing off a joint, my friend. Love you, buddy.

Some of our best highs came while cruising around or just sitting in a car with the windows rolled up. The smoke never left the car, and the high was non-stop, it seemed. When smokin' and tokin' while driving a car, you tended not to hit the joint, but you still got wicked high anyway, as the smoke from the joints was everywhere and never left the car.

Finally, something good about secondhand smoke.

Not often, but sometimes, our high brought on *"life."* The group could never be larger than two when it came to this, as three or more were just too many voices to hold a sane conversation about our lives.

Luckily, the only person I ever went to life on a regular with was Joe, though I did do a few with Tina and a few with Nick, as he would talk about being the father of girls later in life, his hopes for their lives, some of his regrets, and his hopes for the future.

The night grows darker in the vast land of Tex-ass. The clock's hands have reached their peak, marking the passing seconds as they now begin their descent toward the early morning hours.

Memories of a poignant encounter with Nick flood my mind, accompanied by the haunting melody of "See You Again," a heartfelt tribute to the late Paul Walker, who met a tragic end in a fiery car crash back in November 2013.

The music softly plays in the background, intertwining with my thoughts, transporting me back to that vivid moment atop Great Hill Park, overlooking Wessagusset Beach.

Closing my eyes briefly takes me back to a vivid memory, where I can almost taste the aromas of the pot, feel the gentle breeze on my skin, and hear my dear friend speaking passionately about life. Although this occurred around 1995, it remains eternally imprinted in my mind, a moment that will forever linger within me.

The sun is slowly leaving the sky as the warm breeze of the Atlantic pushes its way up Great Hill. Again, music, memories, and the love of a dear friend have brought me back to such a special moment. I am standing next to the flagpole in the grassy area of the parking lot atop the hill. There are only a few cars here now, as it is still light out and the fun doesn't really start until the sky has grown into darkness.

In the parking lot, my gray Z-28 Camero stands silently, accompanied by a blue Mustang. As I approach the cars, a wave of nostalgia washes over me, for I know what is about to unfold. Leaning against the Mustang, a figure emerges from the shadows, smoking a joint. It's Nick, a familiar face from years gone by.

Joining Nick by the car, I, too, lean against it, accepting the joint he offers. In those moments, Nick reminisces about his family, sharing stories and memories. It's bittersweet to see him again after all this time. "It's good to see you, Nick," I say, cherishing the connection we once had. We continue our conversation and smoke until the night sky is adorned with stars and the distant Boston skyline shimmers with lights.

It's been a long day
Without you, my friend
And I'll tell you all about it
When I see you again

Every time Joe and I embarked on these meaningful moments in life, it would consistently start with Joe saying, "You know, Trace." And from that point, we would delve into profound discussions about our dreams, aspirations, hopes, and, inevitably, worries about life.

. Joe and I would often see our futures as uncertain, but the more we smoked, the clearer things became, and we always managed to find solutions to our discussions in some sort of deep-thought fashion. *Never really made any sense the next day when we weren't high.*

Joe and I were masters at discovering the most peculiar spots and people with which to indulge our recreational activities. As I previously recounted in this literary masterpiece, there was this one occasion in the mystical realm of Mattapan Square, precisely at the bewitching hour of two in the morning. Our journey commenced at the esteemed establishment known as Fathers 2, where we engaged in some intense libation consumption. If my memory serves me right, it was situated on

Beacon St. (although the details have become somewhat hazy over time). On that fateful night, they were offering pitchers of beer at a bargain price. Although the quality of the beer left much to be desired, it did possess the magical ability to chill one's soul and provide a delightful buzz.

I'm not really sure how we got there in the first place, but there we were, standing at the last stop of the Green Line, smoking a couple of fat ones with some of the locals of the square at 2:00 A.M. I am still not really sure how we made it home after that. I am guessing we smoked until the 5:00 A.M. train took us back to Boston and then took the Red Line to Quincy and the East Weymouth bus home to the Moreland Rd. stop. Then it was a quick walk to Joe's house, where we crashed until the next night and went right back out again.

As we grew older, our challenges transformed, encompassing everything from navigating romantic relationships to excelling academically—and even my personal encounter with home-lessness while Joe pursued his passion for music. Undeniably, Joe possessed and continues to possess extraordinary talent. Yes, Joe was and remains incredibly gifted when it comes to music.

Whenever I spent time with Tina, it was usually filled with peaceful moments and brief conversations. Our interactions mirrored our personalities, with Tina being one of the kindest people I have ever met.

Her voice is like that of an angel, capable of transform-ing any song into something enchanting. It's amazing to have another friend with such incredible talent. *"Yes, another friend who is that good."*

Larger groups, *"Forget about it."* Off we would go, on music, sports, ragging on each other, and every dumb thing we could think about. Never once did any of us go, *"Ohh, I forgot,"* and giggle. But then again, we never did sit in Red's cellar and pre-tend that we were smoking pot for a television show.

If anything, *at times*, pot brought out some very in-depth thoughts about life. But the high was always remembered and never lost in the smoke of the *"duh."*

How I wish I could go back to Weymouth in the seventies, where we hung out at each other's house or the ball field, having a buck suck. If you don't know what that means, you're not from Weymouth. A bag of weed for thirty bucks. Everybody chipped in a buck, and we rolled the bag. We'd get about forty jays. Oh, those were the days. ~ John W.

It seems, at least to me, that the days of smoking have come to an end. I still remember every high and every moment of laughter that came with these moments. I also remember my days back in the day. Some were happy, but many were sad and lonely. Toking and friendship did help me through many of these times. Heck, those times helped us all.

It's time to move on from this chapter. As we stroll down the memory lane of our upbringing in Weymouth, each chapter adds to the story of our past. Every memory holds the key to countless others, all woven together by the significant moments that shaped our lives. As I reflect on those years, I can't help but feel a sense of nostalgia and longing. The memories of carefree days spent with friends, dancing to the rhythm of the times, are etched in my mind. The seventies were a time of exploration and self-discovery when we forged our identities and embraced our individuality.

Twenty, twenty, twenty-four hours to go
I wanna be sedated
Nothin' to do, nowhere to go-oh
I wanna be sedated
Ramones, "I Wanna Be Sedated"

Our story continues. ~ trace

Chapter Twelve

The Weymouth Drive-In

Intermission—You Look Like You Could Use a Snack

The Weymouth Drive-In, which opened on Thursday, May 28, 1936, proudly claimed the title of New England's first open-air theater. Interestingly, it was the fifth drive-in to be constructed in the entire United States. Situated on the western side of Bridge Street (State Route 3A), just north of the bridge leading to Hingham, this establishment could accommodate up to six hundred vehicles, attracting visitors from Weymouth, Hingham, and Quincy. However, its existence came to an end in 1964 when it was demolished to make way for a new twin-screen drive-in. Each screen could hold eight hundred cars. Unfortunately, this new venture was short-lived, closing its doors in April 1976.

I do remember being squeezed under the back seat of the family station wagon in my younger days, along with my brother Rick, as we entered the drive-in. My parents needed to save the money, I am guessing. The whole time, my mother would be silencing us, "Shhhhhhh," as my father pulled the car to the main booth to pay the entrance fee. "Two, please," he would say, and then once we passed through the gate, my mother would give us the "all clear," and my brother and I could come out of hiding from under the seat.

I'm not really sure how many movies we saw as a family unit, but I do remember a few, such as *Zulu* and *Dragnet*. Once, there was a huge thunderstorm, and the power went out in the whole area. We were issued rainchecks for another time. I'm not sure if we ever went to see the show.

When I was younger, I never got a chance to drive to the Weymouth Drive-In because it closed around the time we all got our driver's licenses. However, I did go to the Braintree Drive-In on a few different dates. Usually, Joe and his girlfriend at the time would accompany me and whoever I was seeing. Most of the time, Joe and I would just chat while the four of us smoked a lot and barely paid attention to the movie we were supposed to be watching with our dates.

"Trace, we are all heading up to catch *Woodstock* at the drive-in tonight," Joe called out as I got to the neighborhood. Yes, the movie that would shape an entire generation and beyond was playing, and it would be one of the few times that hundreds of youths would not be drunk, high, tripping, and stupid all around the drive-in that night. The movie, billed as "three days of peace and music," transfixed us. To this day, the festival was arguably the single most profound event in the history of music.

The moment the sun disappeared from the sky, we settled on the cozy pavement of the drive-in parking area. Our eyes were fixed on the crowd above on the screen, a multitude of half a million individuals—hippies, dreamers, and seekers—all coming together at Max Yasgur's farm. From August 15–18, 1969, the stage loomed like a sacred platform, ready for the musical legends to take their place. Max Yasgur's farm in Bethel, NY, became the meeting point for musical acts from various parts of the world. A staggering number of young people assembled harmoniously at Woodstock, the largest congregation in a single location ever recorded. The impact of Woodstock on music and American culture remains palpable even today. Interestingly, it was being showcased at the Weymouth Drive-In.

This film captures the unforgettable moments of the renowned music festival held in 1969 at a field in Woodstock, NY. The organizers were unaware that attendees would defy the boundaries and transform the event into a celebration of love and music. From Richie Havens's powerful rendition of "Freedom" to Jimi Hendrix's iconic performance of the National Anthem, certain acts have become legendary and continue to resonate with audiences even today.

> *Look what's happening out in the streets*
> *Got a revolution, got to revolution*
> *Hey, I'm dancing down the street*
> *Got a revolution, got to revolution*
> ~ Jefferson Airplane, 1969, Woodstock, "Volunteers"

The atmosphere at the drive-in was electric, with the crowd erupting in cheers and shrieks as Jefferson Airplane took the stage and launched into their hit song "Volunteers." This particular track was relatively unknown to most of us on the East Coast, but that didn't stop us from being instantly captivated by the incredible talent of the West Coast band.

As the night unfolded, we were treated to an unforgettable lineup of artists who had performed at Woodstock, including the likes of Richie Havens, the Grateful Dead, The Who, Joe Cocker, Santana, and many others. This movie screening became a symbol of the transformative power of music during that era, representing a revolution that was happening right in our own town of Weymouth. It was a true testament to the arrival of the seventies and the cultural shift that came with it.

In the future, after a span of twenty-five years, a father who is raising his son alone decides to embark on a trip with his eleven-year-old child. Their destination is an open field named Winston Farm, located just west of Saugerties, New York. The purpose of their journey is to attend an event known as Woodstock Two, which promises two additional days filled with peace and music. My dear son, I hold a deep love for you. However, the details of this particular tale shall be shared in another instance, within the pages of a different book. ~ Dad

Back in the day, before the gang had cars, the only way to watch a movie was by sneaking into the drive-in theater. We had a few options to get in, but we all thought that the Rez was the ideal spot. The chain-link fences were always broken, so it was simple to enter the place as long as we avoided getting caught by the cops.

The Rez, short for the reservoir, was a hidden gem nestled on the outskirts of town. It was a place where we could escape the monotony of our everyday lives and immerse ourselves in the magic of the silver screen. With no cars of our own, sneaking into the drive-in theater became our thrilling adventure, a rite of passage for our mischievous gang.

Once we were inside, it felt like we had complete freedom to wander around and relax. We usually entered the Rez through Elva Rd., Frank Rd., or Julia Rd.

These paths led to a trail that led up a steep hill. Once we made it to the top, a lengthy gravel road brought us to the rear of the screens at the drive-in, where we could discover entrances to the parking lot and freely explore for excitement and entertainment. However, you never brought your beer along but, instead, hid the drinks in the woods outside the Rez's fence. It would be impossible to run with a case of beer if the police were chasing you, and you didn't want a neighbor to spot you and inform your parents. This would result in you being grounded and embarrassment for your parents.

I don't really remember going to the drive-in for any movie other than *Woodstock*. It was just a popular spot for teenagers to gather and hang out in the warmer months.

I have a clear memory of a night when about fifty kids were wandering around the drive-in, looking for a group of out-of-town teens who were rumored to have attacked a local kid from Weymouth, possibly over drugs or a girl.

It seems like a few of the tougher kids in the crowd were planning to confront and fight the group of out-of-towners while the rest would support the locals. Luckily, I never felt the urge to join those who sought trouble. Don't get me wrong; the gang could stir up some trouble, but engaging in fights was never our thing.

Just to make it clear, while the group from the neighborhood could create disorder, we always chose to handle disagreements and disputes in a non-violent manner. It's funny when I reflect on it because, besides going to see *Woodstock*, the gang hardly ever went to the drive-in together. Instead, we were happy just hanging out in our peaceful neighborhood, getting high, and chatting about music and sports all night.

Mary and I sat together one spring evening, leaning against a speaker pole, her head resting gently on my shoulder. It was a moment filled with warmth and comfort, a memory I hold dear in my heart. At this point, we had become a real couple and spent most of our time together.

As the movie commenced, she drew nearer, intertwining our heartbeats in a moment of shared intimacy. This movie had such an impact on us, as the seventies were all about true love and rebellion.

Reflecting on the moments spent with Mary, it was undeniably a love story straight out of the seventies. Our fashion, sitting back to back on the grass, sharing conversations, and passing a joint back and forth—all painted a picture of the small yet significant dramatic moments that defined our relationship.

The movie was *Aloha, Bobby and Rose*, which came out in 1975. It greatly influenced my future as a writer in ways I never expected. This film showed me how music can be used to create powerful storytelling moments, making me see how it can elevate the impact of a story in a book, not just in movies.

As the amazing blend of visuals and music in *Aloha, Bobby and Rose* filled our hearts and souls, this made me realize something important: that music has a special power to bring out feelings, memories, and experiences in a way that no other art form can.

Years later, this discovery inspired me to explore the endless ways music can enhance my storytelling, as in *The Neighborhood Gang* and other books about life I have written and will write.

I just recalled watching a Salem witch trial movie at the drive-in one night, and it was extremely disturbing. They used pliers to pull out a man's tongue and subjected the accused to other gruesome tortures to force them to confess as witches. Of course, I didn't stay until the end of the movie.

Even today, years later, I usually choose to leave before the end of the movie since I tend to avoid films that exploit torture and pain for the sake of audience discomfort. Too much of that is already in the world.

Joe told me the other day while we chatted about the drive-in and our times there that he worked in the concession stands there for a few summers.

"Gotta tell ya, Joe, I don't remember ever seeing you at the concession stand working. I am guessing it is because I was also working up the street at the pizza joint on Bridge St."

Reflecting on the past, I now understand that the drive-in held a deeper significance for us teenagers in Weymouth. It represented not only a venue to watch movies but also a symbol of our freedom and independence.

Within its walls, we could break free from the constraints of our daily lives and fully immerse ourselves in the enchanting realm of cinema, surrounded by our companions and the gentle summer breeze.

The drive-in provided a sanctuary where we could truly be ourselves, liberated from the pressures and expectations of the outside world.

Whether we indulged in substances, engaged in altercations, or simply laughed the night away, the drive-in offered an array of experiences that extended far beyond a mere evening at the movies.

In essence, the drive-in provided us with a space to truly immerse ourselves in the magic of our teenage years, cherishing every single moment.
~ trace

But I'm near the end, and I just ain't got the time
Oh, and I'm wasted, and I can't find my way home
~ Clapton & Winwood, "Can't Find My Way Home"

And our story continues ~ trace

Chapter Thirteen

The Rez

The Rez and Great Esker Park coexist as one place, forever linked yet distinct, each holding onto the echoes of the past that once defined them. Despite their differences, these two places are forever linked by the land they share and the stories that intertwine their pasts. The echoes of the past can still be heard in the wind that rustles through the trees, the songs of birds that fill the air, and the laughter of children playing down on Julia Rd. Park on the ballfield.

~ trace

The Rez, formerly known as the Hingham Naval Reserve, served as a significant provider of U.S. munitions from 1903 to 1961. Spanning 990 acres along the Weymouth Back River, this depot played a crucial role in supplying ammunition. The locals of Weymouth affectionately referred to it as "the Rez," a shortened version of its original lengthy name.

In 1960, my family relocated to Weymouth from Germantown in Quincy. I have vivid memories of attending kindergarten at the Pilgrim Congregational Church on Athens St., right across from Beals Park. I can still recall the journey back home daily from the daycare in a gray station wagon, with no seatbelts to secure us kids in the far back.

I also remember my brother Rick and I strolling up the Rez when I was just a young child, probably around four years old. We made our way up the ninety-foot hill and then walked down the gravel road at the top, heading toward the Hingham Bridge. During this walk, we came across a breathtaking view of the Back River for the very first time, with the Hingham Munitions Base visible across the bay. I distinctly recall that the base appeared to be closed, as there was no sign of any activity there.

A few years later, my brother and I decided to embark on a little adventure. We hopped onto our inner tubes and paddled our way over to the base, where we indulged in some exploration. We even had the thrill of jumping off the docks a few times before we eventually made our way back to the Weymouth side of the Back River.

Rick and I used to wake up early in the morning, around 3:00 A.M., on Saturdays and Sundays during the summer and other vacation weeks. We had a routine of going to the Hingham golf course to work as caddies, earning six dollars a day. To get there, we would walk through the Rez and cross the Hingham Bridge, which took us about two hours. Our goal was to be among the first in line to get a caddying job, although we were never first. However, being in the top five meant that we usually managed to start our day on the course around 9:00 A.M.

Rick, being older and larger than me, always had the advantage of being chosen first for carrying the golf bags. It seemed that most golf bags weighed over forty pounds, and many golfers believed I was too small to complete all eighteen holes, especially considering the uphill journey, which seemed never-ending. However, I always managed to prove them wrong and complete the task. At the end of my twelve-hour day, I would earn around five to six dollars, depending on the golfer's game.

During the summer and after school in the warmer months, some of us in the gang would hike up to the Rez and make our way down the gravel road to the underside of the Hingham Bridge. It was a popular spot for teenagers of all ages to hang out on the big sloping granite slabs by the water. Eventually, we would climb up the side of the bridge and take the leap, jumping about forty feet into the Back River from the girders below the bridge.

Climbing up the side of the bridge was no easy feat, but it was a challenge we reveled in. Our hands gripping the rough concrete, our feet tiptoeing along narrow ledges, we ascended like daring mountain climbers. Our hearts pounded in sync with the rhythm of our steps, adrenaline coursed through our veins, and an indomitable spirit pushed us closer to the edge. Standing on the girders below the bridge, we'd stare down at the water below as its surface shimmered in the sunlight. The leap we were about to make evoked both fear and exhilaration, a duality of emotions intertwined with the embarrassment of being called a chicken by your friends who had already jumped or the satisfaction of *"All right, trace! Ya did it!"* when you finally made the plunge.

I remember only two people ever diving from the top of the Hingham Bridge. From the girders to the top of the bridge was maybe another fifty feet, and the thought of jumping from there was always: *If you jump from the top, you will break your legs or even die, so you must dive.* "Ahhhhh, nope," was the general reply. Amongst the young and brave of Weymouth, diving wasn't a feat of more than five feet at best.

Through the passing years, Rick and I joined forces on numerous occasions. We dedicated ourselves to tidying up the sandy shores of Weymouth beaches as part-time summer employees. The sun kissed our faces during the summer days as we cleaned beaches and ballparks. We also embarked on the task of cleaning dishes at Harts Caterers in Dot, ensuring every plate was spotless and gleaming. During baseball seasons, we transformed into champions of beverage sales at Fenway, quenching the thirst of passionate Sox fans. Not limited by season, we even braved the winter cold to sell fresh vegetables at the bustling open market in Haymarket Square, nestled in the charming North End of Boston.

The reservoir was an ideal spot for socializing and, when we were younger, playing with toy guns. Once a group of approximately ten children formed into two teams, one team would be granted a ten-minute advantage to hide and strategize their ambush up the hill. Endless disputes arose as the concept of magical bullets ensured that no matter how the makeshift gun made from a stick was fired, you were considered "dead." Consequently, we spent hours tirelessly pursuing each other all around the area of the reservoir. To this day, I am pretty sure that some of my best times as a youngster were spent up on the Rez.

In my isolated writer's retreat in Tex-ass, I find solace in the gentle melodies that permeate the chilly night air. The haunting tune of "The Night They Drove Old Dixie Down" by The Band, from their iconic performance in *The Last Waltz*, resonates deeply within me. As I listen, my thoughts drift to my beloved older brother, Rick, who is slowly succumbing to the clutches of dementia. It pains me to know that he resides in a squalid bed tucked away in a dimly lit room within the depths of a nursing home, grappling with the horrors of his deteriorating mind. Rick, I am filled with profound remorse, and if I were granted a single wish by a higher power, it would be to trade places with you, sparing you from this desolate existence.

Virgil Kane is the name
And I served on the Danville train

'Till Stoneman's cavalry came
And tore up the tracks again

And our story continues. ~ trace

Chapter Fourteen

Great Esker Park

"The initial murders are shocking, and the presence of an unknown entity lurking under a popular park is wonderfully disturbing... Hints of a promising Hitchcockian thriller."
~ Kirkus Reviews

Weymouth's largest open space is Great Esker Park, established in 1966. The park's standout feature is the Esker, a winding ridge that runs alongside the Back River. Standing at a height of ninety feet, it holds the distinction of being the tallest esker ridge in all of North America. This unique formation was created twelve thousand years ago when a glacier retreated, leaving behind massive boulders in House Rock Park. Although the name changed, locals still affectionately refer to it as "the Rez," much like how people continue to call the New Boston Garden by its original name, *the Garden.*

As we grew up, the Esker became a trendy destination for weekend parties during the sunny summer season. If you weren't in the mood for the drive-in, you could always join a bonfire gathering in the hollow and enjoy the scenic view of Whale Island. I can't remember a single instance when the police appeared in that vicinity, so the parties carried on smoothly.

On the other hand, going to the drive-in had its moments of dodging the cops as you tried to enter before it was time. And you could never bring in your case of beer, so you needed to hide it in the deep brush of the Rez and hope no one took it.

Back in the day, it was a regular occurrence for us to explore the thick vegetation near the rear entrance of the nearest cinema to the reservoir. Our purpose was to smoke marijuana, enjoy a drink, and simply pass the time. We always made sure to enter when night had fallen and the movie was already underway. Upon reaching the dense undergrowth, we would crawl a little further towards the center, where a small, open space awaited us, ideal for around ten people to gather and experience a heightened state of mind.

Whenever I needed to escape, I always managed to get away with ease, confident that no police officer could catch me if I had enough space to run. I believe the authorities never seriously attempted to catch some of us, although I suspect there were a few individuals they constantly watched out for. However, I won't delve into those details, as that happened years ago and most of us have matured since then.

"Feats, Don't Fail Me Now" ~ *Little Feat*

Jean and I had been dating for more than a year, and our love journey led us to the Esker. On the weekends, her curfew had been extended to midnight, which allowed us more time together. Interestingly, my boss at the pizza joint would secretly gift me a bottle of Boones Farm Wine, saying, *"Enjoy yourself, but remember, you didn't get this from me!"*

Around seven o'clock, I planned to collect Jean, and then we'd make the thirty-minute stroll back to Julia Rd. Park. There, I had hidden the Boones Farm Wine in the underbrush.

We would grab it and swiftly make our way up to the Esker and down to the hollow, where we'd enjoy our first drink.

Throughout the night, we found ourselves laughing and engaging in conversation, constantly fending off pesky mosquitoes and other flying bugs that relentlessly bothered us in the dense forest of the Esker. With half a bottle consumed, we knew that reaching first base was inevitable, although our encounters were often cut short due to the insects' lack of understanding of romance. We were too preoccupied with swatting ourselves to truly enjoy any baseball-related activities.

As for the ideal spot to progress further, that would be behind Bicknell if transportation was not readily available, but that story will be saved for future pages.

I've mentioned multiple times before that Jean and I never reached the neighborhood because I wanted to maintain a clear distinction between my real life and my true self, which I concealed. I'm not sure if this explanation makes sense to anyone else, but Joe, Jim, and Mark understand exactly what I'm trying to convey. Our friendship has withstood numerous challenges, and I am grateful to have them by my side. Thank you, guys, for always being there for me when I needed your friendship.

> *Well, I've got to run to keep from hidin',*
> *And I'm bound to keep on ridin'*
> *And I've got one more silver dollar*
> ~ The Allman Brothers Band, "Midnight Rider"

Without a doubt, the large gathering of local teens down in the valley overlooking Whale Island resembled scenes from *Lord of the Flies*, a novel written by William Golding. With a large bonfire burning in the center of the valley, the nights were filled with drinking, drugs, sex, and fights and would be some of the most memorable times any of us ever had up on the Rez.

Parties at the Rez never had formal invites; they just seemed to spontaneously occur through word of mouth. Without cell phones or social media, news of the party would spread to hundreds of Weymouth teens, who would journey up the steep mountain and down into the valley to attend a night of drinking and drugs.

The Rez held countless experiences for the youth of Weymouth over our teen years, where we explored love, indulged in drinking and drugs, and ventured into various other endeavors. It served as an escape from the chaos happening outside its boundaries, providing a space for both intimate and lively gatherings with bonfires, cheers, conflicts, heartbreaks, new romances, and countless other occurrences. It was the epitome of coolness for the youth of Weymouth, setting the stage for future generations. The Rez was and is unique, and we fully embraced its essence.

As I sit here writing, memories flood my mind, intertwining with each other and evoking a sense of nostalgia. It's a fascinating experience, like a journey through time, where music and memories merge. The present moment feels like it's around 1972, and it's incredible how an American songwriter's prediction has become a reality, emerging from the shadows and into the spotlight.

Lou Reed's "Walk on the Wild Side" takes us on a journey into the lives of people living on the outskirts of society, specifically within New York City's underground scene. This song celebrates diversity and serves as a testament to the countercultural spirit of the 1970s, all while being accompanied by a captivating and unforgettable melody.

Candy came from out on the island
In the backroom, she was everybody's darling
But she never lost her head
Even when she was giving head
Lou Reed, "Walk on the Wild Side"

As the sun dipped below the horizon, darkness descended upon the Esker, shrouding it in an eerie silence. Park Ranger Ryan Gallagher, haunted by the unknown entity that prowled the land, felt a chill crawl up his spine. Determined to uncover the truth and put an end to the mounting casualties, he ventured deeper into the heart of the wilderness, where the secrets of the Esker awaited him. ~ *Esker*, a horror, thriller, suspense book written by a storyteller from Weymouth, Massachusetts, D.L. Tracey

You don't know when you've got it good
It's getting harder
Just keeping life and soul together
~ Nik Kershaw, "Wouldn't It Be Good"

And our story continues. ~ trace

Chapter Fifteen

Wessagusset Beach

Researching Weymouth blew my mind! Turns out, this town was home to a bunch of badass Pilgrims who ditched Plymouth and made Weymouth their new kickass haven, where they could live life on their own terms. Some things never change; even today, Weymouth is a kickass city.

Wessagusset Beach derives its name from the settlement established in 1622 by Thomas Weston. A marker located at Great Hill Park illustrates the strained interactions between European settlers and indigenous tribes during that period. Originally erected in 1923, the marker was re-dedicated in 1998, emphasizing the triumph of Myles Standish and fellow settlers over native leaders like Wituwamat and Pecksuot. Standish has traditionally been celebrated as a hero in Plymouth Colony, yet it is crucial to recognize his detrimental impact on the native tribes in the area during European colonization. The 1623 Massacre at Wessagusset exemplifies this, as Standish led members of the Neponset band of the Massachusetts tribe into a trap, resulting in multiple fatalities. Standish's actions were driven by suspicions of a conspiracy against the colonists, particularly involving Wituwamat, although scholars have not found any evidence to support this claim.

When I think about Wessagusset Beach, memories flood back, drawing me in like the ebb and flow of the tide. I find myself retracing the steps of my past, walking along the shore in solitude, reminiscing about the beginning of my journey in young adulthood. And even today, on my trips back home, I return to this old place and walk and remember.

I have fond memories of Mom reminding Dad to obtain the annual beach parking permit. We would load up our trusty old blue and white station wagon before making our way to the beach for swimming lessons. Eventually, as I got older, I would just be dropped off to spend the day there.

It wasn't until I reached the age of nine that my mother granted me the freedom to stroll down to the nearby beach by myself. She assured me that it wasn't too distant and instructed me to return home once the streetlights illuminated the neighborhood,

Unbeknownst to me, this would signify the end of my treasured moments with her, as my beloved mother was embarking on a new chapter of her life with another family—one that involved non-stop beating of me. However, Joe, in his wisdom, advised me to let go of that tale and leave it untouched for another time.

Sweet days of summer, the jasmine's in bloom
July is dressed up and playing her tune
And I come home from a hard day's work
~ Seals & Croft, "Summer Breeze"

The lifeguard station, situated at the edge of the beach, marked the transition from the old to the future new beach, with a lengthy stroll along the jetty connecting the two shores. The station of brown wood on stilts, with a large opening at the front for the lifeguards to keep a look out on the beach, resembled what you'd see on *Baywatch*, complete with life-guards sporting white paste on their noses and the typical orange lifeguard swimsuits.

I took swimming classes for three summers, and I passed the lifeguard class years later when I was around sixteen or so, but I never followed through with that.

As time passed, the beach transformed into a haven for tranquility, seclusion, endurance, and beyond. I had outgrown childhood, yet adulthood still eluded me. Although I was a teenager who understood certain aspects of life, the essentials remained out of grasp. Education was a distant memory, as math could not sustain a homeless teen. Geography did not offer protection to a homeless teen. Science did not offer direction to a homeless teen. History did not feed a home-less teen.

Whenever I visit Weymouth, I make my usual stop at the beach. As I sit on the shore, looking out at the endless ocean, I can't help but reflect on the struggles I faced as a home-less teenager. Surprisingly, the beach played a pivotal role in shaping me. It cultivated my inner strength and resilience, sparking a flame of optimism and determination that couldn't be snuffed out. Each day, I face life head-on, embracing chal-lenges with the motto "Living the Dream."

Yeah, running down a dream
It never would come to me
Working on a mystery
~ Tom Petty & The Heartbreakers "Runnin' Down A Dream"

And our story continues. ~ trace

Chapter Sixteen

McCulloch Grade School

Welcome to grade school
As a child, I remember the days when we walked to school
without our parents, joined the Cub Scouts, and felt a sense of
independence. We would line up in a straight line, ready to
march into school, and had to raise our hands to ask for
permission to use the bathroom. Sometimes, we would even be
kept after school because our handwriting wasn't perfect. The
pressure from our classmates would increase if we got scolded
by the teacher.

Attending elementary school during the 1960s was a unique experience filled with both challenges and memorable moments. The classrooms were often lined with neat rows of wooden desks, where students sat facing the front of the room. The curriculum focused on the basics of reading, writing, and arithmetic, with a strong emphasis on rote memorization and repetition. Teachers were strict, and discipline was enforced through punishments such as standing in the corner or writing lines. Despite the strict environment, there was a sense of camaraderie among classmates, and recess was a cherished time for playing games like tag or jump rope.

Overall, attending elementary school in the 1960s provided a foundation for learning and social development for most of us. And then there was me and my times at McCulloch School.

Family stature seemed to be important to the other kids on Frank Rd. back in the early days. The neighbors to the right of our home had a very mean girl who must have been a sixth grader when I started first grade at McCulloch School back in 1963.

Does anyone recall the safety patrol stationed at intersections to help children cross the street? One of these patrols happened to be the neighborhood girl known as "Bigfoot," who enjoyed making me wait while other kids crossed. Once everyone was gone, she would tell me to wait and then leave me behind. One day, my brother Rick discovered this and reassured me that Bigfoot had no authority over me. He informed our dad, who then visited the school and had Bigfoot removed from her safety patrol duties, and the brutality she seemed to enjoy inflicting on me came to an end.

During the next six years, I made my small neighborhood bigger by exploring it after school. My friendship with Joe was growing, and Jim had moved into the neighborhood a street behind us, attending the third grade of our local school. A few other kids on the block also went to McCulloch, and we tended to walk the fifteen minutes to school together every morning.

When it was time for school to get out, I always went back to Frank Rd., where I felt safe with my friends from the area. But things started to change as I made new friends in class and our friendships grew stronger during recess.

Throughout the years, friendships have come and gone in a constant ebb and flow. Reflecting on my life's journey, I can recall various companions from different chapters of my life.

Some friendships may have faded, yet there are those special few with whom, despite the infrequent encounters, I always effortlessly pick up where we left off. Regrettably, it is a rarity to maintain connections with college or even elementary school acquaintances. I have been lucky in this matter, as all my friends from grade school are still my friends today.

As the final bell rang on the last day of elementary school, a bittersweet feeling washed over me. I had spent countless hours with my classmates, forging memories that would last a lifetime. We had laughed, cried, and grown together, but now it was time to embark on a new journey. The transition to junior high was both exciting and intimidating, as we would be leaving behind the familiar hallways, faces, and teachers we had grown accustomed to.

The year was 1970, and as my time in McCulloch school ended, new friendships and social bonds started to form, setting the stage for the Bicknell Junior High chapter.

The summer days signified the conclusion of many childhood adventures, and many beliefs were about to be shattered. They also foreshadowed the thrilling and nerve-wracking beginnings that were waiting at Bicknell Junior High School, just a thirty-minute walk from the neighborhood.

Reflecting on it now, the summer of 1970 holds a special place in our hearts as a pivotal moment in our lives. It signified the transition from the carefree days of our childhood to the challenging journey of adolescence.
~ trace.

And our story continues. ~ trace

Chapter Seventeen

Bicknell Junior High School

"The best thing about being a teacher is that it matters. The hardest thing about being a teacher is that it matters every day." ~ Todd Whitaker

Thank you, Mr. Mullen. Because of you, I am a teacher.

We braced ourselves for a whirlwind of change as the small groups of graduates from each school—McCulloch, Saint Jerome's, Johnson, Wessagusset, and Athens—were about to explode into a massive influx of approximately three hundred new students. Familiar faces would soon be replaced by a sea of unfamiliar ones as everyone from the five elementary schools was about to come together for the daunting journey of seventh grade at Bicknell Jr. High School.

Gone were the days of carefree laughter and innocent friendships that had defined our time in elementary school. We were embarking on a new chapter in our youthful journey, one that promised growth, challenges, and a deeper under-standing of the world around us. Bicknell Jr. High School was the gateway to adolescence, a place where we would forge new connections, discover our passions, and navigate the complexities of teenage life.

I entered room 111 with a mix of excitement and nervousness, unsure of what the new school year would bring. As I settled into my seat, I looked around at the familiar faces of my classmates from the previous year, realizing that we were all in the same boat—entering a new grade and a new chapter of our academic journey and lives.

I listened intently as my new homeroom teacher introduced herself and outlined the expectations for the year ahead. The transition from being at the top of the social hierarchy in sixth grade to now being at the bottom in seventh grade was daunting, but I was determined to make something out of all this. After a quick explanation of the bell and how long it took us to move from one class to another, I was given a slip of dot-matrix computer paper with the class, the room, and the teacher, as well as the time class started. Boom—the bell rang. "I will see all of you at the end of the day, as you must come back to homeroom before you leave for attendance," the teacher called out as we all ran to the door, not wanting to be last to the next class. It seemed boot camp had started.

Throughout the day, I, along with nine hundred other kids in three grades, navigated the hallways of the large building, trying to find our way to each class and adjust to the new schedule. As I passed by older students in the corridors, I couldn't help but feel a sense of awe and admiration for their confidence and maturity.

That night, I reflected on the ups and downs of the first day of seventh grade. While the transition was challenging, I knew that with time and effort, I would find my place in this new environment. I was ready to embrace the challenges and opportunities that seventh grade would bring, knowing that this year would be a stepping stone to my future growth and success.

Talk about being wrong—this was not at all what would happen in my case.

Making my way to the entrance every morning, I couldn't help but notice the groups of students huddled together, puffing away at their cigarettes as if it were a normal part of their daily routine. Some were engaged in animated conversations, while others stood in silence, lost in their thoughts.

It was as if smoking had become an integral part of their social interactions, a way to bond and connect with their peers. What struck me the most was the lack of fear or concern among these students. Many teens smoked openly, without any worry of being caught or reprimanded by the school authorities.

> *Them good ol' boys were drinkin' whiskey and rye*
> *Singin', "This'll be the day that I die*
> *This'll be the day that I die"*
> ~ Don McLean, "American Pie"

The gang was a saving grace during the initial days of Bicknell. Granted, we'd started our group only three months ago, but having familiar faces to talk with in the halls or sit with during lunch and hang out with on the way to and after school made a big difference.

I was lucky to make friends with Joanne, Russell, Bill, and Jay in Bicknell. They eventually became my closest friends and classmates, which was pretty cool. Surprisingly, the neighborhood gang and I didn't have the same classes or get to eat lunch together much while we were in Bicknell. Most of the gang was a year ahead of me in school, so our paths never really crossed unless we passed each other in the hallways on our way to other classes.

During the lunch periods, I found myself sitting and chatting with classmates I had never really interacted with before. It was a great opportunity to make connections with people outside of my usual social circle and learn about different interests and backgrounds.

This helped me expand my social skills and become more comfortable meeting new people. Overall, the changing lunch periods at our school provided a valuable chance to broaden my social circle and develop new friendships, some of which have lasted a lifetime.

Joanne and I still chat often, even after several decades since our time at Bicknell.

However, the gang made sure to hang out after school and on weekends. Our bond grew even stronger as we explored the small town together, finding hidden spots and creating inside jokes. We were each other's support system, always there for one another through the good times and the bad.

Bicknell introduced me to the concept of hot lunches, which was a new experience for me. During grade school, I used to walk home, eat lunch, and then return to school, all within sixty minutes.

However, at Bicknell, leaving the premises was not allowed, so students either had to bring their own lunch or purchase it from the cafeteria.

As I settled into this new routine for the next three years, I began to appreciate the convenience of hot lunches. No longer did I have to worry about packing my lunch every morning or rushing home during the short lunch break. Instead, I could simply head to the cafeteria, choose from the array of options, and enjoy warm fish sticks or Friday pizza right there in the school—or stand in line for an ice cream sandwich.

Without the convenience of cell phones, students relied on face-to-face interactions in the cafeteria, gym, study period, and hallways to stay connected with their friends and class-mates.

On the first part of the journey
I was looking at all the life
There were plants and birds and rocks and things
~ America, "Horse with No Name"

It was a time when conversations flowed freely, laughter filled the air, and friendships were strengthened over shared meals. The cafeteria was not just a place to eat but a hub of social activity, where kids made plans for that night and the weekend, gossiped about who liked who, and asked one another if there would be any fights after school.

Of course, so many memories were made, and relationships were nurtured. It was a simpler time when the art of conversation and human connection were valued above all else.

I spent most of my lunches with Bill, Russell, and Jay. We would sit at the end of one of the massive, long tables in the cafeteria. Most of the tables seemed to be segregated by gender, with the boys sitting together, ragging on and throwing food at each other or across the cafeteria, and the girls bent over, whispering to one another.

Remember people setting off cherry bombs or M-80s in the school during class? We would all hear a loud BOOM and just start laughing.

Showering after gym class was mandatory at Bicknell. However, the shower area lacked individual stalls, so we had to shower together.

If anyone refused to shower, they would receive a detention. To avoid a full shower, many of us would simply wrap a towel around ourselves and quickly wet our hair under the shower head.

This trick usually worked, as the teacher would assume we had showered. But there were times when our gym coach stood there and observed thirty thirteen-year-old boys hurriedly shower, dry off, and get dressed, often still wet for their next class.

Bicknell's gym classes were designed to push students to their limits in various sports, and the gym teacher introduced a new challenge in each class. Typically, the classes focused on the current season and the sport being played by the school team.

As the school team's season progressed, Bicknell's classes became more focused on the specific sport being played. Students would work on drills and strategies that directly related to the upcoming games, helping them to better understand and excel, and if they did, the student would be offered a spot on whatever team was playing at the time or on other teams as they came into season. *"Go maroon and gold!"* we'd cheer, the colors of Bicknell uniforms.

Bicknell had a full range of all-season sports. Football and cross-country were in the fall. The winter months brought hockey and basketball. In the spring, track and field and baseball were the sports.

I've been going through the responses on the Bicknell Junior High Group on Facebook, trying to remember how long our classes were and how much time we had between them to avoid being late. None of the group members seem completely certain, but most agree that classes were around forty-five minutes and we had about three to five minutes to get to the next class.

Some members mentioned that they used to strategically plan their routes between classes to avoid the crowded hallways and make it to their next class on time. Others reminisced about the bell system that signaled the end of one class and the beginning of the next, prompting a rush of students to move quickly to their next destination in a stampede.

Any who dared to arrive tardy or lacked the will to partake in a particular class needed to beware, for the sinister hall monitor awaited, poised to demand your pass with a spine-chilling, ghastly voice that echoed, "PASS, PLEASE."

The regular school dance, which took place every few months on a Friday night, emphasized the importance of socializing, as it allowed us to interact with the opposite gender in a school environment.

I can't recall all the bands that performed, but we never had a DJ, and the music, like us, was vibrant and filled with emotions like hope, fear, sadness, drugs, and pure rock.

Our teachers and parents didn't realize how quickly these gatherings introduced us to the growing drug scene in Weymouth and nationwide.

While drinking was still the primary source of amusement at these school events, incorporating "The Boo" took things to a whole new level, introducing us to the concept of being completely intoxicated and adding the term "wasted" to our new and growing vocabulary.

Memories flood back as I gaze at my computer screen. I vividly recall the days spent in classes at our junior high school. The bustling hallways between periods made it feel like a challenge to navigate, yet somehow, we always made it to our next class just in time. Pausing to use the restroom, I would often encounter five students smoking while one kept watch and signaled that *it was safe*, ensuring that they weren't caught by a teacher entering the bathroom.

Smokin' in the boys room
Nah, teacher, don't you fill me up with your rule
'Cause everybody knows that smokin' ain't allowed in school
~ Mötley Crüe, "Smokin' in the Boys Room"

I have a vivid memory of attending the Bicknell prom with a tall blonde girl who happened to be my friend in a few of my classes. However, describing the night as a disaster would be an understatement; it was far worse than that.

Initially, my brother was supposed to be our chauffeur for the evening, taking us to the prom and then to dinner at Valle's Steakhouse in Braintree. Unfortunately, just moments before we were about to leave, she called and informed me that her mother and a friend would be driving us instead.

The evening was a blur of awkward conversation and uncomfortable silences. By the time we finally made it back home, I was relieved that the night was over. Looking back on that disastrous prom night, I can't help but laugh at the absurdity of it all.

It may not have been the magical evening I had hoped for, but it certainly made for a memorable experience. And having dinner after the prom over at Valle's Steak House was lots of fun. I had the steak and clams plate. Add a baked potato, and I was there. I wish her mom had smoked, as a joint would have really hit the spot.

As time passed and we embarked on our individual journeys, the memories we shared in Bicknell continued to hold a special significance in our hearts. Despite attending different schools and residing in different cities, the connection we forged in that quaint town will forever remain cherished in our lives. The friendships I cultivated and the moments we shared in Bicknell will always hold a special place in my heart. ~ trace

I was born to run
I was born to dream
The craziest boy you ever seen
~ Loverboy *"Turn Me Loose"*

And our story continues. ~ trace

Chapter Eighteen

Weymouth North High School

The final chapter of my youth education had arrived. I boarded the bus for the first time, on my way to North Weymouth High School. This was the place where we were supposed to reach new heights in our education. The next three years were meant to prepare us for adulthood and advanced studies. However, things didn't quite turn out as planned for me.

My high school experience was a complete disaster from the start. Being homeless made it impossible for me to focus on my studies, and having to juggle work, food, and basic survival left no time for attending classes. Detentions piled up, I missed school regularly, and passing any of my subjects seemed like an impossible feat.

After some time, I decided to pursue my education and successfully completed the General Educational Development Test (GED) while in the Marines.

A couple of years later, I enrolled at Wichita State University with the goal of becoming a special education teacher.

Throughout the years, I continued to attend university to enhance my writing abilities, and I still do. However, I can't help but feel a sense of regret for missing out on the high school experience and not being able to share those moments with my classmates.

After one and a half years at Weymouth North High, I was officially a ninth-grade dropout as I never completed even the first year with all my detentions and missed classes.

In my second year, I was granted a work pass so I could leave at noon and head to work at the pizza joint, but I was told that for the rest of the year, I had to sit on the office bench until 3:00 P.M. to make up for last year's detentions, a full half hour after school let out. Needless to say, I couldn't do any of this and dropped out three months into the second year. But there is much I remember from the time I was there.

Long lines to the big, round dining hall. I am not sure, but I think there were six lunch lines in the cafeteria.

Some students now had cars and needed to park in back of the school and over by the vocational side. I remember there were so many cars that some were parked on Middle St. in a long line in front of the school.

If you didn't drive, finding your bus below the cafeteria in the parking lot could prove quite a problem. The big yellow buses seemed endless as they waited for the wave of students to fill them for them for their rides home.

I recall the entire school being summoned to the auditorium a few times a year for reasons that I didn't pay much attention to. We were all just thrilled to be out of class.

It's incredible how the entire school, even with the vocational wing, managed to squeeze into the seats while the teachers stood like guards along the walls and doors.

The gym stands could be pulled out, and the whole school could fit, mainly for building team spirit through rallies for the sports teams.

Every Saturday morning, I would make my way to Legion Field to watch the maroon and gold football team fight for the school's honor. The band played non-stop, creating an electrifying atmosphere.

Na-na-na-na, hey, hey, hey, goodbye
Na-na-na-na, na-na-na-na, hey, hey, hey, goodbye
~ Paul Leka, "Na Na Hey Hey Kiss Him Goodbye"
This song is forever a football stadium song.

It only cost fifty cents to enter the game, but if you didn't have the money or simply didn't want to pay, there were approximately ten different ways to sneak in. Personally, my preferred method of unauthorized entry involved scaling the chain-link fence at the back left side of the stadium and leaping twelve feet down to the ground, all while avoiding the barbed wire that adorned the top of the fence.

Team and school spirit were considered significant aspects of school culture back in the seventies. Team jackets were a sign of greatness. Hand-drawn team spirit signs were everywhere on the walls, and the talk was always about the next big game. *Every game was a big game.*

Fight, maroon and gold
We'll cheer you on
Let's go!
And it's fight, fight, fight with all our might
Let's go maroon and gold!
Thank you, Richard C., for the school football fight song.

Despite our mutual interest in sports, the other members of the gang never bothered to join any high school teams. We believed that it would eat up our precious smoking time, and none of us liked Miller Light beer.

I, on the other hand, did give it a shot and managed to make it onto a few of the school teams. Unfortunately, circumstances in life prevented me from actually practicing or playing.

Thinking I could pick it up effortlessly, I took French as my language requirement. I envisioned myself fluently conversing with native speakers and immersing myself in the rich culture of France.

However, my aspirations were quickly shattered when I started taking the class. The initial excitement soon faded as the complexity of the language hit me like a tidal wave.

Turned out I could not speak French, so I thought, *Let's try Spanish next year.* I learned to speak Russian and sign language in college, and I am pretty good at both of them.

In science class, we had to dissect a baby pig, which was an experience that left me perplexed and overwhelmed by the unbearable smell. As the teacher handed out the scalpels and gloves, I couldn't help but question the purpose of this activity. I had no desire to become a butcher.

Why did we have to dissect a baby pig? What could we possibly learn from this gruesome exercise? These thoughts swirled in my mind as I reluctantly approached the lab table. The moment we made the first incision, an overwhelming stench filled the room, assaulting our senses and making it difficult to concentrate. The pungent odor of formaldehyde mixed with the distinct smell of decaying flesh created an atmosphere that was both nauseating and unforgettable. Yes, I was not going into the medical field or becoming a butcher at a local supermarket.

Math has always been an area where my abilities have fallen significantly short, to say the least. So, when my wife, a remarkable individual who is tenaciously pursuing her constitutional law degree at Harvard despite her age, approached me with a question from her quantitative reasoning class, I found myself utterly perplexed.

The problem's incomprehensibility left me with no choice but to offer a feeble and obscure retort: "Call Paul."

For me and the rest of the students in this specific math class, it felt like a complete waste of time, often ending up as a noisy study session. I have blurred memories of trying to study algebra while engaging in conversation with a stunning girl seated in front of me.

I never did get the math, but I did date this girl for a few weeks during the summer that year—until one of the gang members convinced her he was a better date than me. One reason I never brought a girl to meet the gang was that most people back in the day were a better date than me.

The teachers shouldn't be blamed for any of this, and the failing reports they sent home didn't matter because there was no home to send them to. It's crazy—I even got detention just because I couldn't get those letters signed.

Looking back on this, I am sure no one at school could fathom something of this nature happening to me back then, so why try to explain this to the teacher?

I never really took the time to tell them why their reports were not being signed, and when Cotter suspended me until my mother showed up at school, which she never did after a week, I just went back to school and was never asked again to have a report signed. I'm thinking they called my parents and were told, "Sorry, he doesn't live here."

North Weymouth High was truly one of a kind, and the town deserves recognition for its forward-thinking approach. The vocational school at Weymouth North focused on equipping students with practical skills. They learned trades like mechanics, printing, sheet metal work, carpentry, and many others. Interestingly, the vocational school even produced some top-notch bong pipes and roach clips.

The halls of Weymouth North offered a profound learning experience to all who attended this remarkable institution of learning. Your education was there; you just needed to grab it.

I recall the days when we could freely smoke cigarettes outside the cafeteria during lunch breaks and between classes at Weymouth North. While this may seem like a trivial detail, it actually provided a valuable growth opportunity for many students who attended this esteemed institution.

It seemed that every hallway wall was covered in lockers for the students. When classes were changing, the hallways would become a sea of kids running around like squirrels.

The lockers acted as temporary pit stops where students swiftly spun the combination locks, causing a mechanical symphony of clicks and clacks to fill the air. In one fluid motion, textbooks were exchanged with practiced precision and repositioned. The occasional locker door would slam shut, with the reverberation punctuating the constant motion surrounding it.

We were always shouting and jumping around, trying to catch a glimpse of who was coming down the hallway. Since we didn't have cellphones, we had to quickly make plans for after school or lunch during the short breaks between classes.

In the past, school breaks were a time for students to socialize and engage in face-to-face conversations with their peers. It was a chance to step away from the demands of schoolwork and enjoy some time to relax and recharge. However, with the rise of technology, these moments of real human connection have been replaced by quick texts and instant messaging.

Your everlasting summer, and you can see it fading fast
So you grab a piece of something that you think is gonna last
~ Steely Dan, "Reelin' in the Years"

It's truly astonishing how much we accomplished within the limited time we had. Gym class, in particular, taught us valuable lessons in time management.

On sunny days, we would swiftly make our way to the gym lockers, change into our sports attire, and head out to Legion Field for a fast-paced game of softball or touch football. If we forgot our sneakers, we would walk laps around the track field. After a short while, we would return to the gym, take a quick shower, and rush to our next class. All total, I think class time was forty-five minutes from bell to bell.

From sports teams to academic clubs, this school truly had something for everyone after school. Whether you were interested in art, music, or science, there was a club or class available to cater to your interests.

The teachers who led these activities went above and beyond in their dedication to helping students succeed. They sacrificed their time and energy to ensure that students had the resources and support needed to excel outside of the traditional classroom setting.

I do remember going to the gym on Fifties Night with a few friends. We got high and drank before the dance and then pretty much just stood against the gym wall, never really having any nerve to ask a girl to dance.

High school relationships felt like the real deal. Now that we were older, with jobs and cars, curfews were pretty much non-existent since our parents had stopped bothering to enforce them, trusting us to make responsible choices.

I never got a chance to participate in many of the activities associated with the high school scene. I would have loved to join many of the clubs, and I was quite good at sports.

But in hindsight, I think the things I most wish I hadn't missed were graduation day, going to the prom, and having my picture in the yearbook so that, years later, I could look back and reminisce about my years at Weymouth North—not to mention the friendships left behind that never had the chance to grow into more.

I don't attend reunions because I did not graduate. I would have loved to head off to college the next year and start my teaching years earlier than I did.

The word on the street is that the 1975 prom was quite eventful and had a lasting impact on future proms. However, it's important to remember that this is just hearsay and may not be entirely accurate. But it wouldn't surprise me—or any of us.

Ah, the sweet taste of confidence after thinking I had conquered all the valuable lessons school had to offer. Little did I know that life had a different plan in store for me. It decided to reveal its true complexity just to keep things interesting. And, of course, the true depth of my knowledge could only be uncovered with the passage of time because who needs instant gratification anyway? Time, the ultimate revealer of my strength, wisdom, and endurance, or lack thereof. How delightful. ~ trace

I've been first and last
Look at how the time goes past
But I'm all alone at last
~Neil Young, "Old Man"

And our story continues. ~ trace

Chapter Nineteen

And the Beat
Goes On

The rock concerts in Boston and New England during the 1970s hold a special place in our hearts. The atmosphere, the excitement, the sense of rebellion—it was a unique time in history. From Kenmore Square to Yarmouth Coliseum, the venues echoed with the sounds of rock music and the essence of that era. Even now, the music from our generation remains a timeless treasure, passed down to our grandchildren, who embrace it as their own. ~ trace

The conclusion of the 1960s marked the downfall of the "Bosstown Sound," which was deemed a significant disappointment from the start due to being criticized by the media as "establishment hype" at its lowest point.

Personally, I have never bought into the idea that the Boston music scene faltered in the 1960s. On the contrary, the city, known for its beans, teemed with musical talent and witnessed a period of significant musical advancement and creativity during that era.

As the 1960s progressed, Boston became a hub for emerging rock bands and musicians, drawing in crowds from all over the region. Venues such as the Boston Tea Party and the Psychedelic Supermarket became iconic spots for live music, hosting legendary acts like The Velvet Underground, The Doors, and the Grateful Dead.

Local bands like The Remains, The Barbarians, and Ultimate Spinach gained national recognition, contributing to the city's reputation as a breeding ground for talented musicians. The Boston Sound, a unique blend of rock, folk, and blues, emerged as a defining characteristic of the city's music scene.

The energy and creativity of the Boston rock scene extended beyond the city limits, influencing neighboring towns on the North and South Shores. Fans flocked to clubs and bars in places like Cambridge, Somerville, Hull, Marsh Vegas, and Quincy to catch up-and-coming bands and experience the excitement of the burgeoning music scene.

The 1960s marked a turning point for Boston's music culture, setting the stage for the city's continued influence on the rock 'n' roll landscape in the decades to come. The era of rock music in Boston was a time of innovation, collaboration, and unforgettable performances that left a lasting impact on the city and its surrounding communities.

> *I'm m gonna tell you a story*
> *I'm gonna tell you about my town*
> *I'm gonna tell you a big fat story, baby*
> *Aw, it's all about my town*
> ~ The Standells, "Dirty Water"

Rock music continued to gain popularity in Beantown during the 1960s, causing a buzz in nearby towns on the North and South Shores of Boston. The city was gearing up for its inaugural rock 'n' roll era of the seventies. *And let me tell ya, we weren't disappointed.*

As Aerosmith and the J. Geils Band neared their moments of glory, soon to be followed by Boston and The Cars, they would be joined on the journey by so many more great bands, both at the local level and around the world. The city was ready to keep the music alive and continue the fight of rock 'n' roll.

> *Every time that I look in the mirror*
> *All these lines on my face getting clearer*
> *The past is gone.*
> `~ Aerosmith, "Dream On"

Yes, the past of the sixties was gone. The seventies brought a new meaning to music, and that was called rock in New England and around the world. Yes, rock was out of its infant stage and hitting its teen years, with all of us grabbing hold and heading for the future of music.

So much was going on in our lives as the seventies came upon us. As we left the safe structure of the sixth grade for the classrooms of Bicknell High School, drugs, the opposite sex, and the war became real concerns for most of us. Our once pure and innocent world suddenly became infiltrated by the allure of these mind-altering substances, casting a shadow of uncertainty over our choices and friendships. But music, sweet music, was everywhere.

Thinking back to my personal concert experiences kinda of puts me in a daze about them days. But it was September 1973, the old Boston Garden was the venue, and the concert was Jethro Tull's *A Passion Play*.

Boston Garden. Numerous Jethro fans often regard this tour as a pinnacle of artistic expression for the band. And yes, I was there with Jean. Though we were no longer dating, I had asked her to accompany me a few months before and talk about getting high. Yes, we were way past high.

> *In the shuffling madness*
> *Of the locomotive breath*
> *Runs the all-time loser*
> ~ Jethro Tull, "Locomotive Breath"

Jean and I never got high together while we were dating. We did drink a bit and took a trip on blotter once, but that was the extent of it. However, her new boyfriend was affiliated with the Beal St. Gang, who often hung out behind the church on Beal St., and getting high there seemed to be the norm. Jean seemed to enjoy getting high. At the concert, she disappeared for about thirty minutes with a guy she met on the way to the bathroom and came back totally wasted.

> *Love how Ian Anderson kept his flutes in a very old wicker*
> *baby carriage.*

One of the most notable concerts to ever play at Boston Garden was an American guitarist, songwriter, and singer. His career lasted only four years, but he is considered one of the most influential electric guitarists in popular music history, as well as one of the most celebrated musicians of the twentieth century. Three months after playing the Garden, he died of a supposed drug overdose. That man was Johnny Allen Hendrix, known to the music world as Jimi Hendrix.

> *It's old age, and it's wisdom*
> *It whispers, "No, this will be the last"*
> *And the wind cries*
> *"Mary"*
> ~ The Jimi Hendrix Experience, "The Wind Cries Mary"

My first laser show was Kansas's *The Point of Know Return* at the Boston Garden. I went with a few friends, and we were just nine rows from the front. At the end of the concert, after all was said and the music done, the band just yelled out:

"Good night, Boston. Were Kansas."

Government Center. It was August 1975, and Harry Chapin was playing outdoors at the center. The Summer Concert was sponsored by "The radio station known as WRKO." In the sixties and seventies, this radio station played top-forty music—yes, on the AM dial, as FM was still in the growing stage and didn't take over the airwaves until 1978 in the Boston area.

Around this time, I was carrying most of my belongings around in a backpack or leaving stuff at the gas station I was working at, as my home life was non-existent and movement seemed to be the only thing keeping me alive. With the exception of Joe and Jim, I kept most of this to myself.

Music helped me get through these times, and I needed this concert by Harry Chapin to make it through the day. Walking out of the Government Center T stop, I found myself in a huge crowd of Harry fans. I was almost embarrassed by my youth and backpack, but no one seemed to care as I made my way to the front of the massive crowd.

And there he was, sitting on a chair flanked by a small band of fellow musicians, and I was forty feet away. For the next few hours, I listened with my eyes shut, getting lost in this man's music and recharging my resolve to make it through another day.

So, I go on my way, trying to forget I'm alone. ~ trace

My child arrived just the other day
He came to the world in the usual way
But there were planes to catch and bills to pay
~ Harry Chapin, "Cat's in the Cradle"

The Rathskeller, affectionately known as The Rat, was more than just a music venue—it was a cultural hub for the Boston music scene. Located in Kenmore Square, The Rat was a gritty, no-frills club that attracted both up-and-coming local bands and established acts from around the country. The venue's intimate atmosphere and reputation for showcasing cutting-edge music made it a favorite among musicians and fans alike.

The Rat's stage saw countless legendary performances over the years, with bands like The Cars and the Pixies getting their start at the club. The venue's eclectic lineup reflected the diverse tastes of its patrons, with punk, new wave, alternative rock, and metal all finding a home on The Rat's stage. The club's reputation for fostering emerging talent helped solidify its place in Boston's music history.

My memories of past nights at the Rat were hazy, but tonight felt like a new experience. I held off on drinking until the crowd filled in, sitting close to the stage with a beer in hand, anticipating my friends' arrival, but they never showed up.

A few people filled the seats around me. A quiet young couple sat a few feet away as the band took the stage. They delivered an incredible music-driven performance that left me mesmerized despite not knowing who they were. The venue came alive with their music, leaving me in a totally sober awe.

Boston's very own The Cars took the stage, delivering a visually chaotic performance that left us mesmerized. Their musical prowess was unparalleled, flawlessly blending smooth melodies with an enigmatic charm. The small crowd was captivated in a state of pure awe.

I don't mind you comin' here
Wastin' all my time
'Cause when you're standin' oh so near
~The Cars, "Just What I Needed"

The atmosphere crackled with energy as The Cars performed, each song adding to the excitement of the musical experience. The small but vocal audience joined in, their voices harmonizing seamlessly with the band's, creating a memorable and emotional concert.

The Cars' exceptional talent soon became the talk of the town in Boston's music community. Their music had a universal appeal, captivating listeners from various walks of life. As their popularity soared, the media took notice, featuring them on magazine covers and ensuring their songs were constantly played on the radio.

No one will ever shut the "F" up about The Rat. And for good
reason—from '74 to '97, it defined Boston rock music. ~ trace

Despite its rough exterior, The Rat was beloved by many for its sense of community and camaraderie. Fans would line up around the block to catch a show, and the club's regulars formed a tight-knit group that supported each other and the bands that played there. The Rat's legacy lives on in the memories of those who experienced its magic firsthand, and its impact on the Boston music scene can still be felt today.

Welcome to the Grand Illusion
Come on in and see what's happening
Pay the price, get your tickets for the show
~ Styx, "The Grand Illusion"

Orpheum Theater. In the fall of 1977, my date and I were at one of the oldest theaters in the United States, catching the band Styx. I gotta tell ya, the end of the alley at 1 Hamilton Pl. is a pure music zone. The seating was small and cramped, like on an airplane, but who cared? We stood the whole time.

> *Oh, I used to be disgusted*
> *Now I try to be amused*
> *But since their wings have got rusted*
> ~ Elvis Costello, "(The Angels Wanna Wear My) Red Shoes"

The Paradise Theater, currently called the Paradise Rock Club, can be found on the outskirts of Boston University. It's a popular spot for students from various prestigious universities in Boston. The venue is owned by the Don Law Company, a significant player in the Boston music scene that also oversees the Boston Garden and the Cape Cod Coliseum.

It was December 1977, and my date and I found ourselves knee deep in snow, eagerly waiting in line with tickets in hand to see The Attractions, a group from England. Little did we know that this band was actually just the backing band for the talented new wave musician Elvis Costello.

Time has not diminished my admiration for Elvis Costello's music and the raw passion he brings to every note.

In my personal ranking, Costello stands head and shoulders above all other guitarists of the seventies, one who left an indelible mark on the history of rock and roll.

I attended multiple concerts in Boston at various locations, including performances by Kansas, Blue Oyster Cult, and the Grateful Dead. However, the Grateful Dead's preference for playing thirty-minute songs didn't capture my interest. Fortunately, during the one time I saw them at the Garden, I consumed so many downers that I ended up sleeping through most of the concert—as my friends who accompanied me later informed me.

I had to move
Really had to move
That's why, if you please
~ Grateful Dead, "Bertha"

The 1970s marked a significant period of change and growth for rock music, paving the way for future generations of artists to explore new boundaries and push the genre's limits. The Vietnam War served as a catalyst for powerful protest songs that resonated with the youth and represented their fight against the establishment. Despite the era's uncertainties, it was also a time of remarkable music and indelible moments that still serve as a source of inspiration for artists today.

And it's one, two, three, what are we fighting for?
Don't ask me, I don't give a damn, next stop is Viet Nam
And it's five, six, seven, open up the pearly gates
~ Country Joe McDonald, "I Feel Like I'm Fixin to Die Rag"

On April 16, 1970, a massive gathering of sixty thousand war protestors took place on the Boston Common. At that time, our nation was deeply entrenched in a war with North Vietnam, which had started in 1955 and would persist until April 1975, when America finally signed the peace accords. Over fifty-eight thousand Americans had died when the tally was taken.

I had skipped school that day. I was basically homeless, and the school couldn't call anyone to check up on me, so off I went.

After taking the bus to Quincy, I climbed onto the T and took the Red Line into Boston, exiting at the Park St. T station.

As I ascended the stairs and stepped into the sunlight, I heard the voices of the crowd chanting, "End the war! End the war!" I had learned about the protest from a radio station in the area and decided to take part in it.

The atmosphere was charged with urgency and passion as people from all walks of life came together to demand peace and justice for their brothers and sisters in the war. The thumping of drums beating in unison, combined with chants of "No more war! No more war!" echoed through the commons, creating a powerful symphony of resistance.

Thought I heard a rumblin'
Callin' to my name
Two hundred million guns are loaded
~ CCR, "Run Through the Jungle"

I spent several hours consuming intoxicants, smoking weed, and absorbing conversations revolving around peace and the casualties brought on by the twenty-year war. *"Stop the war!"*

During this time, I had the opportunity to listen to Worcester's own Abby Hoffman, a figure I had heard much about but knew little of his actual words and presence.

As Hoffman was introduced and walked toward to the podium on stage, his gaze was fixed on the Hancock Building towering above the Common. With conviction in his voice, he proclaimed, "Fuckin' John Hancock was a revolutionary. He wasn't no goddamn insurance salesman." Hoffman was right.

Tin soldiers and Nixon's comin'
We're finally on our own
This summer, I hear the drummin'
~Crosby, Stills, Nash, and Young, "Ohio"

While the world may have changed since I first embarked on this journey, my commitment to making a difference remains steadfast. I have witnessed progress and setbacks, victories and defeats, but these experiences have only fueled my determination to continue fighting for what I believe in. I am acutely aware that change does not happen overnight, but I am willing to put in the effort and endure the challenges that come with it.
~ trace

*Don't you know
Talking about a revolution?
It sounds like a whisper*
~ Tracy Chapman, "Talkin' 'bout a Revolution"

And our story continues. ~ trace

Chapter Twenty

Three Songs for a Quarter

Three Songs for a Quarter ~ As I pen the tale of our journey from childhood to adulthood, I stumble upon fragments of memories that don't quite find their place within the narrative of this book. However, each of these snippets holds a special significance for me and all of us, the kids growing up in Weymouth back in the day. They are like cherished melodies, three songs that can be heard for just a quarter, evoking emotions and reminding us of the beautiful moments we shared.

"Hey, Trace, did you play this?" Stevie M. called out in the pizza joint's dining room. He was referring to "Can't You See" by the Marshell Tucker Band. I knew Steve from hockey, though I never got the chance to play with or against him as, back in those days, he was in the elite class of skaters in Weymouth. I worked at this place and was taking a break with a slice of cheese and a Coke.

Turning toward the voice, I saw him sitting with a very hot girl (of course) a few booths over. "Sure did," I called back as the song took us to another place and another time. *"I've gone to buy a ticket now, as far as I can. Ain't a-never coming back."* The song played from the three-songs-for-a-quarter jukeboxes attached to the tables.

"Nice," came the reply from the elite skater.

Bicknell Memories
by
Tina Glover

As a native of California, my transition into the seventh grade as a new student was far from easy. With my parents having grown up in the same area, I felt a certain pressure to assimilate and find my place among my peers. Eventually, I managed to find my way into the inner circle of the "cool kids," and from that point on, we were an unstoppable force. We dedicated ourselves to studying diligently during the day, only to let loose and have a blast once the clock struck 3:00 P.M. Our group had a secret hideaway nestled in the nearby woods, a place that held a special significance for us. We took the time to create a comfortable seating area using logs, ensuring that we had a private space to gather and engage in conversations about life while indulging in our shared love for smoking weed. It was during these moments that we felt a certain magic in the air as if the world's problems were put on hold for a while.

Our bond as friends grew stronger with each passing day, and little did we realize that it would endure for a lifetime. This is how we came to be known as the "Neighborhood Gang."

Back in the day, Liz R. and me, her mom would drop her at my house, and together, we would brave the cold and walk all the way up to Papa Gino's on Bridge Street, where we would enjoy a slice and a Coke! We would sit there as long as we could get away with it—as so many other kids were doing in those days! Liz and I loved Grand Funk Railroad! Those were the songs you would usually hear us playing, especially for hours, with our albums in her room or mine! Oh, to be able to go back in time, if only for a day, to reunite with all the kids from North Weymouth and beyond! ~ Mary J.

My husband sings, "With a purple operator and a fifty-cent ham"! It should be "with a purple umbrella and a fifty-cent hat." ~ Carol C.

Lee, when I graduated from college, I worked for Papa Gino's. I was a general manager at the Norwood location. We had the biggest dining room in the company. I had about twenty tables with three-songs-for-a-quarter boxes at them. The kids, on Friday and Saturday, would sit at the tables sometimes for hours. I would have to ask them to leave so other patrons could sit down. Well, one young man got irritated and started to punch the box. I asked him to stop, but he punched it harder, broke the glass, and cut his hand severely. I had to call an ambulance. His parents tried to sue me, said I upset him, and that's why he did it. Go figure. ~ Jeff A.

"Trace."
"Yeah, Joe, what's up?"
"I'm so drunk I couldn't hit my ass with a banjo."
"Hmm, I wasn't aware you knew how to play a banjo."

How about waiting for a buyer at Beach Way Liquors on Bridge Street, drinking in the woods underage, and then cutting through Mr. Donut and Burger King in Coral Gables to sneak in the plaza twin drive-in to watch *The Exorcist* when it just came out? Also, Friday nights, jumping on the freight train at Weymouth Heights, jumping off at Lowell Jackson Square behind the bowling alley to party with the East Weymouth girls that we had just met coming from Bicknell to the high school. The good old days. ~ Ken L.

The seventies were fast and slow-paced at the same time. A blur for many of us. It was a magical time with no phones, but word of mouth directed us to follow the crowds with a six pack to a party in the woods. It was a tight-knit community where everyone knew each other and their families and everyone had a nickname. Life was simpler, and memories are sweet. ~ Debbie R.

Back in the seventies, whenever there was a party, invites were always by word of mouth. You had to be in the right place at the right time to hear about it, but our communication skills would have made NASA proud. When I went into the military in 1976, the word spread so far and so fast. My going-away party was broken up by the Weymouth Police and the Massachusetts State Police. I wish it meant that I was that popular, but I knew it wasn't. It was a great sendoff, anyway. ~ Wally P. *You have always held a special place in people's hearts, Wally, and your popularity has never waned. ~ trace*

Oh, the seventies. The music we enjoyed from your own backyard: Joe with The Neighborhood Band, going to the Bell Buoy, Uncle Sam's, concerts at the Garden, and any bluegrass festival within a hundred-mile radius. We enjoyed a variety of artists, from Led Zeppelin, Jethro Tull, and Aerosmith to The Marshall Tucker Band, The Grateful Dead, and The Allman Brothers Band. The best times were the live shows and especially the festivals. Great times, great music, and mainly many great friends. ~ Ginny S.

Weymouth North High School... 1974 & 1975... Weekend gathering at the reservoir...known as the Rez... It would be announced during the week through the hallways of the school. A well-known area behind the Weymouth Twin Drive-In. Always on a Saturday night... There were many ways to get to the Rez from side streets... It was a good walk in the dark to reach the large gully... A road circled the area... A huge bonfire was the main attraction, with at least a hundred-plus kids enjoying themselves with their favorite beverage, simply making great memories!!!! Of course, the best part of the night was when our party was interrupted by the men in blue... Now, that was something!!!!! ~ Jack B.

Legion Field, Mothers of Invention, Frank Zappa. A welcoming, spray-painted entrance to late-night fun. Breaking into the bathroom, turning on the heat under the bleachers on a cold winter's night. I don't know why that particular memory came to me, lol. I always wondered why they never shut the gas off under those bleachers!! ~ Sue M.

I would wear corduroy pants and remember that sound they made when walking. Can't imagine wearing corduroy pants today. But it was popular in high school. ~ Pat M.

I didn't watch a lot of movies back in the day, but a few stand out: *Star Trek IV*, where they want to get the whales back, *Animal House*, *Fried Green Tomatoes*, *My Cousin Vinny*—and a few Clint Eastwood movies. *Animal House* stands apart from them all. ~ Mark C.

Still have all my ABB (Allman Brothers Band) vinyl albums and play them frequently. *Eat A Peach* more than the others, followed by *Live At Fillmore East*, which many rock historians consider the greatest live rock performance ever recorded. ~ Richard G,

I always sang, "Don't fear the reefer," lol, till my grandson said, "It's reaper, Grandma." ~ Vicki F.

I had a monthly subscription to *Popular Science*, *Popular Mechanics*, *Hot Rod*, and *Mad Magazine*. That explains a lot about me today. Lol. ~ Marty R.

I had a few pairs of short shorts in terrycloth. They were so comfy! I can't believe I ever showed that much skin and didn't think anything of it. I sure wouldn't do it now! ~ Linda C.

Walking down the cereal aisle today, Laura and I laughed as we remembered the small variety packs of cereal that you could open from the top, dump in milk, and eat the cereal right out of the box. ~ Lee & Laura

Anyone else remember to dial 16? BT dial a disc service, with a different hit record each week. ~ Rachel D.

There will never be times like the seventies again. I'm thankful we all experienced them. ~ Dave P.

The 1970s were very FAR OUT, MAN!! ~ JC C.

As a seventy-one-year-old man growing up in NC in the early sixties, it was Motown and beach music before the English Invasion. Then came *American Bandstand*, but the real deal was *Soul Train*. I watched *AB* for the hype, but then it was time to get the funk out and learn the latest dance moves for real, then take it to the club that night!!! Thank you, Don C., for all the shorties you helped me pull!!! R.I.P., Mr. Cornelius!!! ~ Gary Y.

Remember when the quadraphonic sound system first came out? Well, we put a mattress on the floor, a speaker at each corner of the room, volume on high, smoking dope, sitting on the mattress, spacing out to Pink Floyd. ~ Shaun F.

The Neighborhood Gang
Tina Glover

It's 6 a.m.
Mom yells for you to get up
Just enough time to put some juice in your cup
Run out the door to catch the bus
Don't forget your books and lunch and meet all your friends
'Cause we're on our way to Bicknell, Bicknell Jr. High
We're on our way to Bicknell, Bicknell Jr. High
It's 3 o'clock
and the bell rings
Already made my plans to smoke some killer weed
There's a special place we like to hang
With the cool people we call the "Neighborhood Gang"
'Cause, we're on our way to Bicknell, Bicknell Jr. High
We're on our way to Bicknell, Bicknell Jr. High
'Cause now were headed down the neighborhood
Where the fun's about to begin
We're headed down the neighborhood
Where everyone will win!
Sunset goes down
Our day's complete
Trace walks you home
So you're not alone on the street
'Cause we're on our way to Bicknell, Bicknell Jr. High
We're on our way to Bicknell, Bicknell Jr. High
Let's hear it for the Neighborhood Gang

Friendships for life
Let's hear it for the Neighborhood Gang
We'll always remain the same
~ Song by Tina Glover

I miss the days of sitting on grass, having fun with friends, getting high, and enjoying life. Those were the best days and the best years of my life. ~ Jean C.

I wanna go back to the seventies and type on a typewriter, untwist a phone cord, and listen to really good music on the radio! ~ Renee C.

The other night, I had a chat with another Weymouth author, Mike Wysocki. He shared a lot of memories with me. Mike who was a bit younger, always recalled how the older kids would run down to the seawall in their jeans and jump into the ocean.

I would so much love to go back to our time. You remember the table jukeboxes that played songs for coins at pizza parlors with Bee Gees in the air? Root beer with ice cubes in plastic tumblers. And a strange sense of relaxation with the music. ~ Rod M.

Blinded by the light, wake up like a douche in the roller in the night.
or
Blinded by the light. Revved up like a deuce, another runner in the night

Remembering school in the seventies, and it was great. Drugs were becoming popular, and we were at the height of the sexual revolution. The miniskirt was popular, and girls were becoming free. The only problem was having to carry a book in front of you all the time. ~ John G.

I love the seventies and cool cars. I had a blue '65 Mustang (my brother put big tires on the back and glass pipes on it). Boy, was it loud, lol. I loved it. ~ Brenda C.

"Don't Squeeze the Charmin."

The park was the best place to go and get high. Didn't need money or nothing, just being with friends and hanging out was everything to me. ~ Josephine V.

Loved getting up early and watching my Saturday morning cartoons. They were the best of the best in slapstick cartoons. ~ Timmy J,

No cell phones, but people actually talking? That phrase "good old days" suddenly makes a lot of sense. ~ Allan G.

Every time we got some change, my brother and I would walk to the corner store for bubblegum cigars and caps for our six-shooters. The seventies were such an easy time to live. ~ Cherie L.

Rattling off the Seventies

Playing with clacker balls... Eddie S. selling me the wrong yo-yo for fifty cents in the seventh grade... Pet Rocks (never had one)... mood rings... TV went off at night... eight-track tapes... Charlie's Angels hairdos... cheese in a can... pull-tab soda and beer... getting up to change the channel... The Dallas Cowboys actually won games... Sea Monkeys... Push-Up creamsicles, balsa gliders... Madge... encyclopedias... not Wikipedia... *Donny*

& Marie... *The Sonny & Cher Show*... *Laugh-In*... *Hee Haw*... and so many more shows... Tang... Lip Smackers... Bobby Orr... Larry Bird... Yaz... Polaroid One-Step... "Gee, your hair smells terrific"... Kool-Aid... *The Brady Bunch*... drinking from the garden hose... ant farms... Sears Christmas catalog... banana seats for your bike... no bike helmets... pretty much no helmets... flower power... the war... protests to end war... wood-trim station wagons... video arcades... Mr. Rogers... the bump...rotary phones... *Star Wars*... *Jaws*... shag carpets... *School House Rock*... Stretch Armstrong... Nerf balls... bell bottoms... big boxes of crayons... *GIVE PEACE A CHANCE... ALL WE CAN SAY IS GIVE PEACE A CHANCE...* crewneck sweaters... "Have a nice day"... Betty Crocker dinner in a box... Radio Shack... Jell-O... *Popular Science*... "Did you watch *Room 222*?"... Horshack bendable figure is such a goofy toy... *Hagar the Horrible, Garfield, Doonesbury, Dennis the Menace, Cathy, The Family Circus, Beetle Bailey*, and so many more comic strips from our youth...

Try and name the shows these catchphrases went with

"Dy-No-Mite!" ... "Ayyyyyy" ... "Wha-chu talkin' 'bout, Willis?" ... "Hey, hey, hey" ... "Nanu, Nanu" ... "Sit on it!" ... "Up your nose with a rubber hose" ... "You big dummy" ... "Book 'em, Danno" ... "De plane! De plane!" ... "Stifle!" ... "Shazbot!" ... "Good night, John Boy" ... "Jane, you ignorant slut" ... "Who loves you?" ... "Kiss my grits!" ... "Lookin' good" ... "Hello...how are ya?" ... "Elizabeth, I'm comin' to join you" ... "Don't make me angry. You wouldn't like me when I'm angry" ... "We are two wild and crazy guys! ... "Just one more thing" ... "The thrill of victory, the agony of defeat ... and so many more we could quote.

Do you remember dot candies? My friends and I would break them off the paper with our teeth. I had a pair of

Maverick jeans covered in a flames design and another pair that had people's faces on them in indigo. Loved them jeans, loved them seventies. ~ Ashleigh J.

Going to Bicknell was a trip in more than one way. I remember everyone smoked cigarettes. We would all light up at the end of the walkway, the curved, chain-link fence. Sometimes, Mr. Cotter, aka Turtle, would try to catch ya lighting up while on school property. Never caught me, though. We were early teenagers doing stuff that is unheard of nowadays. ~ Marty P.

You have got to love it. Going to the beach after school to smoke some pot. Screw homework time to have fun and get high. ~ Dave M.

"'Scuse me while I kiss the sky." Or "'Scuse me while I kiss this guy."

I remember sledding over at the sand pits. The more weight, the faster you went. When you were on the bottom, your nose was right there in the snow the whole ride. That was livin' back in the day. ~ Larry C.

Larry, I remember breaking my nose over there when the sled Jim and I were on ran into another sled, right into my pretty face. ~ trace

"Time to make the donuts."

Lived in the old Dr. Drake house right on the driveway when you come into Bicknell. Remember Cotter, Madden, Ms. Passaro, Loudermelch, Mr. Frado, Mr. Kalishman, Mr. Gaughan, and the Great Ellis Fields. Loved industrial arts. Learned printing, woodworking, carpentry, metalwork, and drafting. I used many of the skills I learned in those classes throughout my life. ~ Mark P.

John B., Dale H., Rosie B., and so many more friends for the summer at the beach. And the music of your time. ~ *Crazy World of Arthur Brown, "Fire"* ~ trace

I wish I had a time machine and could go back to the 1970s. I definitely want to relive 1973, one of the best years on earth. ~ Jackie L.

Yes, we were lucky to live in and experience that magical time. The seventies were great. ~ William T.

Cool, speedy cars, great music, good friends, weed, beers, Saturday football games, Friday night dances at the high school. There was no better time to grow up than the seventies. ~ John S.

"I miss browsing through record shops."

Wicked-hot cars, beautiful girls, Farrah Fawcett hairdos, and love those bell-bottom jeans and tank tops. ~ John L.

Yeah, we had some good times and also some bad times! One of the bad times was when we had the gasoline crunch in the seventies. Long lines on even-odd days for just a few gallons. ~ John B.

Bell bottoms, tank tops, and sandals. No better look. And no better time. Especially the summer of '69. Last days of school and hitting the ground running in 1970. Awesome days. ~ Johnny D.

Live the Term

Make love not war... flower power... keep on truckin'... PEACE... Don't sweat it... Pad... I can't believe I ate the whole thing... Peace out... The man... Stone fox... bummer... too bad... copacetic... down with... fake me out... flat leaver... gimme some skin... hertz donut... jeepers creepers... rip-off... sound as a pound... that was the joint... to the max.. take something to the extreme.

I wish I could take my kids back to that time when life was so simple and real, back to the time when we had a blast!!!! I feel so sad that they will never get the chance to experience that time. SOOO sad that it will never be like that again. But glad for the memories. Thanks, trace, for letting me remember in words. ~ Kathy A.

Maybe it's just because I was born in 1960 and "came of age" in the seventies, but girls back then were smokin' hot and so much more attractive than the girls of today. ~ Kevin L.

Them be da good ol' days! Gone forever, only memories to look back on. ~ Norman B.

For me, it was the music, the cars, the short shorts, your steady girlfriend sitting up so close to you, all the windows of your car open, heading for the drive-in to meet the rest of the gang. Who cares what's playing? You are with your girl, and that is all that counts. ~ Mike M.

When I watch movies that are set in the seventies, there's always something that doesn't ring true. And when watching movies made in the seventies, there is a certain "atmosphere" that can only be found in them. I can't specify what it is, but it can be felt. Same for photos. For some reason, you can see which are genuine and which are staged decades later, like watching a movie and knowing the accent is not a real Baston accent. ~ Tony B.

"There's a bathroom on the right" or "There's a bad moon on the rise"

Sea Monkeys (brine shrimp) were a colossal disappointment for a lot of kids.

I always wore straight-leg jeans—hated wearing bell bottoms. Couldn't stand having all that cloth flapping around my ankles. ~ Jim K.

The wide bell-bottom jeans were great. They kept your boots from getting banged up. Everyone wore them. Great fashion, great music, greatest cars, great friends, great life. Glad to have been alive in the seventies. ~ Rich W.

I had a pair of Peter Max jeans. Every section had a different fabric pattern. ~ Betsy B.

I definitely remember the Pet Rock craze. I can just imagine what Mom and Dad would have said if I asked them to buy me a Pet Rock. ~ Jim G.

I used to have a 1970 Plymouth Fury 383 2bbl 275 horse. And what a rocket. ~ Darrell R

Long, straight hair, add a halter top and then a wide belt, just a dash of flared jeans with four or five patches made the seventies' gal. Yep, that's how I rolled. ~ Chris C

Hanging out, waiting for friends so we could cruise around town. You'll never know what comes your way. We were free. The seventies will live forever with me. ~ Bob S.

Hangin' out down the street, same old thing we did last week and the week before. ~ Mike N.

Give peace a chance. Yes, we truly thought back in '72 we could make a difference; it has been a struggle for sure. ~ Jim W.

Hey, man, am I driving ok? ... I think we're parked, man ~ Cheech & Chong's Up in Smoke

Going to see the Dark Side of the Moon tour, Pink Floyd. ~ Terry S.

Oh, I absolutely loved and devoured *Seventeen* magazine in high school. My favorite was the back-to-school issue. I had a subscription and could hardly wait for the mail to come every month. ~ Tammy T.

"I'm just a sweet transvestite from transexual Transylvalnia, so come up to the lab and see what's on the slab. Ooo, I can actually hear you quiver with antici...pation, but maybe the rain is not really to blame, so I'll remove the cause...but not the symptom!" ~ Tim C., *The Rocky Horror Picture Show*

In the words of Richard Nixon, "Sock it to me."

"Remember these cigarette machines? No checking IDs." ~ Dave E.

"The first time I saw Pong (the first electronic game I ever saw) was at Mr. Cone's Raceway in Fort Worth, Texas, in 1973. It was just a wooden pedestal, flat on top, with a couple of knobs. It had a small screen facing up and a couple of chairs sitting around it. Before that, all we had was pinball, foosball, and pool. Not long after that, electronic game arcades began opening." ~ Terry M.

Have a groovy day!

In 1979, you could fill up a car for $15. Gas prices in the US that year were, on average, 85 cents per gallon.

Breaker, breaker, one-nine

Ten-four, good buddy

Fotomat

National Lampoon

Classic Duncan Imperial Yo-Yo

"Weeble's wobble, but they don't fall down." ~ Rod D.

MAD Magazine

Sharp 'Cuda!

G'night, John-Boy

Did you watch *Candid Camera*?

"Hold me closer, Tony Danza" or *"Hold me closer, tiny dancer"*

"Blue seal in the sky with diamonds" or *"Lucy in the sky with diamonds"*

"'Scuse me while I kiss this guy" or *"'Scuse me while I kiss the sky"*

"There's a bathroom on the right" or *"There's a bad moon on the rise"*

"So, open the door" or *"Soy un perdedor"*

Wow, thanks for so many memories, my friends. From all over the country, from Weymouth to Cali, the moments pour in like a hard rain—of our youth, our times, our memories, our highs, our lows, and so much more.

Unfortunately, as I was in the midst of writing this section, I received the heartbreaking news of my brother Rick's passing. My sister-in-law informed me that he had succumbed to the oppressive grip of dementia and found solace in eternal slumber. Now the words I have penned hold an even greater significance in my heart. I express my gratitude to Rick for the incredible moments of camaraderie we shared and for his unwavering support as a brother. From this point forward, my only solace lies in the cherished memories that will forever linger within me. *May your journey be peaceful, dear brother, until we meet on the other side.*

Dearest Rick, we stood alone today, and I said my goodbyes. We had so many amazing times together. I am now left alone with these memories, but for sixty-six years, I have known, loved, and respected you more than you will ever know. Don´t worry. I've got your family. ~ Rick, I will see you on the other side. ~

And our story continues. ~ trace

Chapter Twenty-One

Here Come the Lost Years

Countless unspoken memories fill my mind, overwhelming it with a myriad of additional moments from our experiences in the 1970s. They must be saved for another day. Deep down, we know that the most meaningful things are often expressed at the end. It's peculiar how people can spend hours conversing without saying anything of substance, only to find themselves lingering by the door of life, pouring out heartfelt words in a rush. It appears that doorways hold the power to reveal the truth of our lives.

Many of the neighborhood gang are not mentioned in this book, mainly because I could not contact them to ask if they wanted to be in it. Countless untold stories lie hidden within the log, waiting to be discovered. Endless tales of joy and laughter that can still fill the night with our highs. The rock star and his companion have countless melodies left to serenade the world with the songs of our past. But amidst it all, nights of emptiness and doubt still lurk in the shadows.

The lost years of the eighties have arrived, dragging me into a dark abyss of drugs and alcohol, leading me down a path of homelessness across the nation. Cocaine and heroin will inter-twine, blurring the lines between time, faith, and any hope for a better future.

And my story continues. ~ trace

Good night, Weymouth.
I'm trace.

Printed in the USA
CPSIA information can be obtained
at www.ICGtesting.com
LVHW041158081124
795950LV00002B/271